Sisters

Hard Times & Brave Women

Sam Bledsoe

Sector 3309 Books

This book is a work of nonfiction. The characters and events described here, the names, and the settings are based on the author's memory of experiences and conversations with the author's relatives in order to portray true life events, many of which occurred in the distant past.

Copyright © 2021 by Samuel Bledsoe.

Front cover illustration, left to right: Mattie Lee, Delores and June

Printed in the United States of America

SECTOR 3309 BOOKS

First United States Paperback Printing: March 2021

To Pamella June—
The daughter who cared for her parents
and the sister who supported her brothers
with a boundless and enduring love
during the trying times of their lives
in spite of the troubles of her own

As God is my witness . . .
they're not going to lick me.
I'm going to live through this;
And when it's all over . . .
I'll never be hungry again.
No, nor any of my folk.
If I have to lie, steal, cheat or kill . . .
As God is my witness,
I'll never be hungry again!

—Scarlett O'Hara
from **Gone with the Wind**
by Margaret Mitchell

Prologue

I have always loved flowers—like roses and peonies that offer brilliant splashes of red and white—flowers that are planted and nurtured in rich, dark soil in neat gardens. There's something therapeutic about working in a garden resplendent with irises, lilies or daffodils in the cool, fresh air of a quiet morning in May.

But there's also something special and serendipitous about wildflowers. Their beauty and color make our world more inviting and pleasant. For example, when I explore a freshly mowed field and spot a purple *passion flower*, it's an unexpected wonder.

And if I happen upon a cluster of stunningly blue or white or purple *morning glories*, I cannot help but think of them as a small miracle. How beautiful and mysterious they are in so many varieties! When the sun goes down they close their blooms and open them again to welcome the morning sun. How they do that I have no idea.

And when I stroll across a sunny glen and happen upon the peculiar yellow *love vine*—not really a flower but a parasitic plant used ceremonially and medicinally in traditional societies around the world—it leaves me baffled yet again. How it got there I have no idea for it reveals no seeds or even flowers.

Most wildflowers are small but some are quite large. Like people they come in all shapes and sizes. There is the tall and very prickly *bull thistle* with its pink tassels, actually edible but not a good choice for cows or man. Don't touch it. And there is the blood-red *trumpet creeper*, a sturdy, aggressive vine often found dominating old fence rows.

Nature offers an amazing bounty of wildflowers, but most of us don't walk the fields, pastures and woods where they are found or even think about them anymore. It seems we don't have time for little things like that. I used to walk by some lots just outside of town that were being readied for building condos. There, before the lawns were graded and sodded, the wild morning glories thrived, small ones and large ones in a variety of colors and eye-catching, orange *butterfly weeds* stood out above the mass of ordinary vegetation.

They are all gone now, able to survive anything but the stubborn advance of human development. In their place stands a monotonous row of condos with neat but boring lawns. May we never become so harried and distracted by the busy lives we lead that we overlook the simple beauty of wildflowers.

Some people are like those wild flowers—they're miracles too— somehow able to thrive in the most impoverished circumstances, thwarted only by the heartless, improvident spread of human civilization.

The three Brittian sisters grew up in the first half of the twentieth century—a most dangerous and turbulent time for America and the world. They endured World War II, suffered through the Great Depression, witnessed the Great Migration of workers from the south and heard about ratification of the 19th Amendment, finally giving women the right to vote. Actually, being able to vote didn't mean too much to them at the time because they were too busy trying to survive.

It has been said that civilization saw more change and progress in the first half of the twentieth century than in all the previous centuries of human existence. That razor-thin sliver of time in the course of human existence witnessed several revolutionary inventions—the airplane, the automobile, the tractor, the radio and telephone, and nuclear energy, for example—that changed the world and transformed human culture. During those years automatic washing machines, refrigerators and other labor-saving appliances gave women in most parts of America an easier life.

But the Brittian sisters grew up in Harlan County in southeastern Kentucky which is situated in the foothills of the mountainous region known as Appalachia. Poverty and isolation were particularly severe in that section of Appalachia which binds together parts of West Virginia northeastern Tennessee, the southwestern tip of Virginia and eastern Kentucky. The poorest people in this region were often families of men like the Brittian sisters' father who worked in the coal mining industry and withstood crippling poverty with few opportunities to better themselves.

These three sisters, growing up in eastern Kentucky during the hard decades of the 30's and 40's, didn't profit much from all the developments and excitements of the first half of the twentieth century.

But they came of age at the beginning of the second half, determined to find a better life from then on. Although full of spunk and flawed like all of us, they made the lives of everyone they touched more pleasant and interesting—until they were treated badly.

I had the good fortune of being related to these three adorable women who were like the wildflowers I came to love. This is their story and in a sense it is the story of all women for every woman is, like those wildflowers, a miracle—beautiful and exotic in her own way.

May we never forget the brave and free-spirited women who are like those ladies of eastern Kentucky, able to survive and even flourish under the most trying conditions and the most difficult of times.

John

J ohn Brittian was born, the seventh of eight children, on June 14, 1884 in Pennington Gap, Virginia. As a child he had a calm disposition and seemed mature for his age. But in 1890, at the tender age of six, he suffered the first of several misfortunes that would stamp upon his personality a serious and melancholy nature; his mother Ella Ball died from an unknown cause. The youngster was crushed.

John's father William was a successful farmer and businessman who owned a boardinghouse. He had neither the time nor the inclination to manage a household of eight children so his fledgling brood was often left to fend for itself. That meant missing a lot of school. Sometimes the neighbors complained that William let his children run wild.

William was a handsome man. Three years after the death of Ella he married Cindy Cadle, a lady he met at church. Together they had two girls and, after that, William paid scant attention to his children by Ella.

John didn't adjust well to the blended family and was often at odds with his new step mother. With two young children of her own, she was not inclined to show him the attention and favor that he had received from his real mother.

Feeling neglected, John became rebellious. He wandered aimlessly around the countryside bitter and angry. His father didn't insist that John get an education so he completed only a few years of elementary school.

The economy of Lee County around the turn of the century depended mostly on farming—growing tobacco—and mining coal. There were few jobs other than manual labor available in the small mines around the rural towns of southwestern Virginia. Without an education, the only work John could find was back-breaking and low-paying manual labor.

John's oldest brother Samuel was successful growing tobacco and, with his father's help, came to own significant tracts of land. He was older and more self-sufficient when their mother died so he adjusted better to his father's remarriage and didn't suffer from the angst and resentment that John felt.

To make matters worse, Sam looked down on his younger brother John and criticized him for what seemed to Sam to be a lack of ambition. Because the two brothers didn't see eye to eye, John got no help from his older brother or the rest of his family.

By the turn of the century, the discovery of vast deposits of coal in eastern Kentucky and the availability of railroads to haul that coal from rural areas to market, created a boom in mining. Wealthy industrialists from the North acquired large tracts of land at cheap prices, opened coal mines, built railroad lines and, out of necessity, camps to attract workers for the rural and sometimes remote coal mines. Between 1912 and 1958, there were over 150 coal companies operating in Harlan County alone.

Initially, inhabitants of these towns were primarily white Americans. But farmlands all over the South were shrinking as inheritances were divided up among the large farm families prevalent in the late 1880s. Subsistence farming became an unreliable occupation so poor whites began leaving the agriculturally depressed states of the rural south in search of a better life. Some came from states like Alabama where they traded the uncertainties of cotton for the hard labor of coal. Some of them found a better life in the coal towns of southern Appalachia.

As the coal industry expanded, it needed more and more workers. The onset of World War I, however, pressed into military service millions of white male workers. The loss of all those workers along with the decline in immigration forced coal operators to hire black migrants from southern states. Consequently, Blacks fled the rural racist south in droves to work in northern industries and Appalachian coal fields.

The coal towns to which these migrants moved were white dominated with blacks and immigrants living in separate, inferior housing, often several families to one dwelling.

Although John had worked for several years in mines around Pennington Gap, he soon realized there wasn't much of a future there. The mines in Lee County were small and didn't pay well, but there weren't any better jobs to be found.

Eventually, John wound up in Harlan County, Kentucky where he heard there were good jobs to be had in mining. It was 1907 and he was 23 years old and the black sheep of his family. He spent about a year shuffling back and forth between Harlan, Williamsburg and Middlesboro, learning the lay of the land and trying to find work.

John didn't care much for religion, but the only place he had a fair chance of meeting a nice girl was at church, so he went to church. One day when he was in Verne, he visited a little Primitive Baptist church and met a pretty young lady named Rhoda Smith. He was immediately smitten by her. It occurred to him that if he didn't find a good job soon, he would lose her to some other fellow with more substantial prospects. He didn't want to work in a big city like Lexington or Louisville and he didn't want to leave eastern Kentucky because he was afraid he would lose Rhoda.

Rhoda was caught in the middle between John and her family. She was from a fairly well off family; her Uncle, "Will" Smith, owned some coal mines and a boarding house. But everyone in Rhoda's family was a Republican, and John was a Democrat who didn't mind saying what he thought of Republicans. That didn't sit well with her parents and extended family who looked down their noses at John. Nor did it help that Rhoda's younger sister Mary didn't think he was good enough for Rhoda and often criticized him behind his back.

For weeks John had been trying to figure out what to do. He was running out of money and becoming desperate; he had to talk to someone. One evening he saw Brian Dunne, a hardened miner he had chatted with several times before, resting on the steps of the small frame house he occupied with his family and smoking a corn cob pipe. Brian's grandfather had shipped over from Cork in 1850 to escape the Irish Potato Famine.

Brian was a wiry fellow with a warm smile in spite of a missing front tooth. He took the last swig from a cracked mug of thick black coffee that had gone cold and coughed. His back ached and he winced when he stood up, but mining is solitary work and he was in the mood to talk. He motioned for John to join him on the steps.

"Did you find y'urself a job now?" Brian asked.

"No, but I've got to get one soon. I've found me a pretty girl I want to marry. I don't want her to get away, but the only jobs I can find are mining jobs."

Brian nodded sympathetically. "Listen, when I was younger'n you are, I was stuck, too. I didn't think I could leave 'cause I didn't have two nickels to rub together. But, I swear if I was you, John, I'd find something else or bust a gut tryin'."

"Why do you say that?" John asked.

"Look, when I was a kid we were too poor for me to get a decent education. I went to school until I was about 10. After that, I helped my paw for a while and went into the mines myself when I was 14. My two younger brothers did the same. We were put into the screen room of a breaker to pick slate. When we were a little older, we went to work inside the mines as driver boys. As we grew stronger, we were taken on as laborers. We worked at that until we could pull our weight as grownups and work in the breasts and gang ways on our own.

"Now there are only two of us boys. My youngest brother Corey lies in the cemetery at Verne—a mountain of top rock fell on him—God rest his soul. He was killed a few months after he took on the job of miner—no more than a month before he was to be married. It was up to me to tell Gracie, his fiancé. She fainted straight away. God, how I hated that. She would have made him a good wife."

He took his pipe and rapped it sharply against the top step. "What are you, John, 22 . . . 23?"

"23," John replied softly.

"I've worked in the mines for half my life but I'm not much older than you." He puffed up his chest and proudly stuck out his chin. "Why, when I was your age, jus' like you, I was strong as a bull; I thought I could handle anything or whup anybody. Why, I could load eight or nine tons a day with the best of 'em."

He exhaled slowly with a rumbling cough and slumped back against the porch. "But the mines will beat you, John. They'll grind you down. I'm 36, but when I look in the mirror, I see a man ten or fifteen years older than that."

He held out his hands and arms for John to see. "Look at these scars and calluses. Look at my gray hair and the worry lines etched in my face. Look how I'm slumped over. The mines will make you old before you know it."

"I've earned as much as most any other man in the mines; yet I barely make ends meet and I'm no better off today than when I started. When our first baby came, as babies are apt to do after you marry, we didn't know if we could make it. There were lots of days when we went hungry so we could feed our baby. Times was awful hard then and they still are."

John didn't know what to say so he shifted his position and nodded his sympathy.

Brian gazed toward the distant mountains and seemed to lapse into a trance. "Let me tell you, John, the mines will kill your soul, too. You work daylight to dark from Monday mornin' until Saturday evenin' under terrible conditions, underground—never seeing the sun. When you come home, you don't have nothin' left for your family."

He fixed his eyes on John again with a hard gaze. "Nobody warned me or things might have been different for me. But I'm warnin' you now. You're gonna' get married—and I'm happy for you—but let me tell you what really kills my soul: when Bonnie sets the table and she's wearin' that same ol' worn out blue dress, 'cause it's the best she's got. She still tries to look good for me but she ain't had a new dress in three years. Sure, she never complains—by God she's a saint! But I'm ashamed; it makes me feel like a whipped dog. What are you good for if you can't buy your wife a new dress once in a while?"

John felt like an iron anvil was pressing on his chest, making it hard to breathe, so he stood up stiffly and stretched. "Brian, sure, everything you say is true but what can I do? I can't get any other job."

"John, if I had it to do over, I'd get the hell out of eastern Kentucky if I had to crawl on my hands and knees. I'd go some place where I could get a decent job, maybe go to Georgia or Tennessee." He perked up. "Hell, that's it! If I didn't have a family, I'd go to Georgia! There ain't no mines in Georgia. Or Lexington. There ain't no mines around there."

He blew out the smoke from his pipe and jabbed his finger at John. "Don't spend the rest of your life like me, down in some dark, damp hole with smoke and dust that will give you asthma and ruin your lungs. Every day you may be blown to bits by a gas or coal dust explosion. Or be crushed to death by a cave in!"

"If somethin' happened to me what man would take on a widow with two kids? Every night I pray Bonnie won't be left a widow with our kids to raise by herself."

John rubbed his temples and the back of his neck wearily. "Sure, I'd like to get away from here but I don't think Rhodie will leave her family."

"John, maybe you ought'a explain to her what kind of life she has ahead of her if you work in the mines."

"God knows I've thought about that. I'm scared she may be expectin' more'n I can give her."

"Well, she probably is." Brian sat back and breathed a sigh. "And there's somethin' else to think about. You may be able to squeak by on your paycheck for a while but eventually some misfortune is going to fall on you. There might be a strike. You might get laid off or get your hours cut back. You might get disabled in a mining accident. Your wife or one of your young'uns might come down with pneumonia or whoopin' cough. When Bonnie had our second child, she had complications and was sick for two months. It took me five years to pay off all the medical bills and we almost starved to death while I was doin' it. We didn't have two stinkin' red cents to our name!"

John had heard enough; he moved to stand up and say good-bye. Just then the front door opened and Bonnie stepped quietly out onto the porch. She was a small, frail woman who, John suspected, like her husband was considerably younger than she looked. She offered a weak smile and sat down by her husband. "I thought I heard my name mentioned," she said.

Brian brightened up and put his arm around her, squeezing her tight as if he hadn't seen her in days. "Bonnie, this here is John Brittian. He's about to take a minin' job and I'm tryin' to talk him out of it. What do you say to that?"

She regarded John with a sweetly sympathetic expression. "I think you ought'a listen to my husband, Mr. Brittian."

Brian thumped John on the shoulder. "There, you see, John, she knows what I'm talkin' 'bout. Like me, my dear sweet wife here was born in a dark, dank holler in Harlan County; she had no hope of getting anymore of an education than me. But she did learn by her dear mamma's hand how to keep house on my piddlin' amount of pay."

He gave her a peck on the cheek. "That's what kep' us afloat."

A cool breeze had picked up and it was blowing his wife's hair across her face. He pulled her closer to him and lowered his voice almost to a whisper: "I was just startin' to tell him about Jack."

Bonnie nodded sadly.

Brian glanced at the distant mountains, gathering his thoughts, and grew somber again. He coughed, a deep rumbling sound from deep down, then turned away from them and spit before continuing. "In 1902, in the fall of that year, not long after Bonnie recovered from her illness, we had another run of bad luck. It happened when coal minin' was in a slump and I was only working about half time."

"At that time, my other brother Jack was workin' his face[1] when he struck a gas feeder. There was a god-awful explosion that slammed him against the face and covered him with several tons of coal. I wasn't working very far from him and, when I realized what had happened, I yelled for help as loud as I could and ran toward him. In minutes a swarm of miners joined me, all of 'em working desperately to uncover him. When we found him, he was horribly burned over his whole body and his laborer lay dead beside him."

Brian's eyes grew moist and his voice cracked. "He was my brother. A good man, I reckon a better man than me. He was single and had been boarding. He had no home of his own. I didn't want him taken to the hospital, so I had him brought to our house where we could look

[1] "Face" - The surface of the coal seam that was dug out, in those days, by pick and shovel to remove the coal.

after him. Besides being burned, his right arm and left leg were broken, and he was hurt awful bad inside. After the doctor got to our house and looked him over, he pulled us aside and said Jack would die.

"But he didn't. By some miracle, he's alive today. And still a miner 'cause that's all he knows. But he lay in bed for fourteen weeks and was unable to work for seven weeks after he got out of it. He had no savings. Eventually I managed to pay all the expenses for his doctors, his medicine, and his living costs."

He looked at John and frowned. "It took a terrible toll on Bonnie here. Lookin' after Jack while I worked wore her out!"

Brian looked at his wife proudly and smiled. "By God, if there ever was an angel, this here's one of 'em. Oh, some people said we didn' have to take him in, that we could have sent him to a hospital or the poorhouse."

"Well, sometimes even God forsakes you; but we are family, John. Who else can you depend on, if not your family? And Bonnie wouldn't have it no other way."

Bonnie seemed anxious to change the subject and tugged at her husband's arm. "Don't forget the strikes."

Brian regarded his wife grimly. "Oh, yes, the strikes. As I said, they'll come along from time to time and you'll have to strike, even though you'll hate to 'cause it's hard to survive while you're on strike. And they may become so violent you get shot or hanged. Or go on so long, your family starves to death. You won't have no choice though 'cause the price of groceries and ev'rything else keeps going up. Ev'rything 'cept your pay, so you have to strike to earn a fair wage to make it."

Bonnie sighed, "He's right, Mr. Brittian. The strikes will ruin you."

Like a deflated balloon, their conversation lapsed into an uneasy silence. What else was there to say? John stood up and shook his hand. "Been nice talkin' to you, Brian. Thanks for the advice." He turned to Bonnie, and smiled, "Awful nice to meet you, Mrs. Dunne."

John thought long and hard about his friend's comments, and he tried even harder to find a better job than mining. But after moving to Grays Knob in Harlan County in 1909, he had no choice. He went to work for the Blue Diamond Coal Company in the nearby community of Chevrolet, a small mining community of about 600 people. He later tried working in other mines such as Black Star and Kits Mining but they were no better.

In 1910 John and Rhoda married when she was 16 in spite of the disapproval of her family. They rented a small house in the Blue Diamond coal camp for about $10.00 per month. Although John was a hard worker, he struggled to make enough money for them to survive.

Year after year, he was barely able to support his family. While he was working at Black Star Mining Company, his jaw was broken and he was almost killed in a mining accident that put him in a Louisville hospital for almost a year. He had no medical benefits or savings.

He was too proud to ask for help from either of their families, although it's doubtful they would have helped anyway. So, out of necessity, Rhoda took in washing from time to time to make extra money.

When John's father died in 1927, his estate was divided between his wife and ten children. John's older brother Sam got control of the estate and finagled the settlement so that John and his other siblings got little or nothing. John was so angry at being cheated that he decided to wash his hands of his family and swore never to lay eyes on them again.

When a miner gets home after working a long day in the mines, he's so depleted he doesn't have anything left to give to his family. After twenty years of back-breaking work in the mines to support himself, his wife and seven children, just as Brian had predicted, John found he was not much better off than when he started.

Unable to work in the mines any longer, John decided to open a small grocery store with the meager savings they had accumulated. But relatives and neighbors took advantage by buying food from the store on credit and rarely paying for it. Consequently, John and Rhoda couldn't live on the small and uncertain income from the store. She, ever the faithful but unhappy wife, took a job. She cooked for workers on an L&N railroad train that traveled around eastern Kentucky and Tennessee.

Mattie, their youngest child and the youngest of the Brittian sisters, was only ten years old then—their other children were on their own—so

Rhoda took Mattie with her. Since they were often gone a week at a time, Mattie missed a lot of school.

But John still didn't have enough capital for the business and it failed. Too many of his customers didn't pay their bills.

Over the years, the strains on their marriage intensified. Sometimes they fought bitterly but divorce was not an option for Rhoda. John was withdrawn and depressed because he was getting older and he knew his health might fail at any time. Rhoda retreated more into her church activities for some hope of a better life. Church remained her only social outlet and her faith was her only solace for the empty, monotonous life she lived.

By the time of the Great Depression the coal towns were already in decline. A slump in the coal industry, the onset of mechanization, and the beginnings of the age of the automobile were all contributing to their demise. The gradual decline of mining over the first half of the twentieth century led to high unemployment and sustained poverty in eastern Kentucky.

By the 1940s, major changes had come to coal mining. Hydroelectric power was becoming more common, and the demand for coal was declining. Mechanization of the mines increased production and made the miner's job easier but drastically cut the number of jobs required. Thanks to the organizing efforts of the United Mine Workers union, gradually miners were paid more, they received benefits and mines were safer. At long last miners had more money and a higher standard of living.

But for John Brittian and many others like him, those changes came too late. He spent all of his working years in the coal mines until he suffered a series of crippling strokes. In 1964, he died at 80 years of age from Black Lung disease, a slow and painful death caused by breathing coal dust for many years. He had no health insurance and he received no compensation during his life for the Black Lung disease. He was a kind and decent man who struggled mightily against great odds throughout his hard life.

After John's death, Rhoda was able to qualify for some Black Lung benefits. She lived on, widowed but never remarrying, spending the last years of her life in a mobile home in Alabama on a lot next door to her daughter Mattie Lee and Mattie's husband Preston Terry. She died at age 97, still resolute in the faith that had sustained her throughout her long and conflicted life.

Perhaps it was by witnessing their parent's own hardships and financial struggles that the three Brittian daughters found the courage to persevere in spite of great disadvantages, never giving up their search for a happier and more secure life.

Rhoda

R hoda Ollie Smith was born the oldest of nine children on October 26, 1894 in Verne, Kentucky in Whitley county near Williamsburg. Rhoda was an attractive young lady, trim and bright-eyed, who dressed better than most women of her day. Her father Samuel was a successful tobacco farmer and his family enjoyed a comfortable life. Rhoda was a good student; she completed high school and was popular with her school mates, although she was shy until she really got to know you.

In eastern Kentucky, the girls married young. In 1909, when she was 15, she met John Brittian, a handsome young man from Virginia who had coal black hair and worked as a miner. She fell in love with him even though he was ten years older than she. He was 6'2" and strong as a bull with a wild streak. He didn't own a car–few people did in 1909–but he owned a horse and buggy. She enjoyed the sense of freedom when he drove her around in it.

She was eager to set out on her own and be free of her strict parents who didn't approve of her suitor. It was obvious to them that he was unschooled, an ignorant and poor coal miner with little future. But to her, he was fiercely independent and a rebel; that appealed to her. Over her parent's objections, when she was 16, she married him on

December 24, 1913, at Stoney Lonesome Church in a coal camp in Norton, Virginia.

Good jobs were scarce in eastern Kentucky and western Virginia so most men had to work in the mines or leave Appalachia. To make matters worse, the Southern Appalachian coal operators owned the mines, the housing, and the company store and usually controlled the politics of the small towns and mining communities nearby.

Her husband found a job in the damp coal mines of the Blue Diamond Coal Company and later in the Kitts Mining Company mines in Harlan. The couple mostly lived in small makeshift houses rented from the mining company. They were typically cramped and roughly constructed structures, one of many in dirty, dusty and sordid projects. She found them depressing, considering what she was used to.

She quickly learned that her parents had spoken the truth: coal mining is a dirty business. Coal is dusty and dirty so coal towns and coal miners cannot be otherwise. The black coal dust settles on everything and anyone within sight.

Before the mines became automated, digging out the coal required hard manual labor under dim, harsh and hazardous conditions. Every evening when he came home around 7:00, he had to take a bath before he could eat. She would have the galvanized tin tub ready for him with lye soap and hot water.

Rhoda knew coal miners had a hard life, but she had not anticipated how difficult it would be to make ends meet. Every month when they sat down to talk about what had to be paid, they had to choose carefully what they could buy and who they could pay. They were always in debt to the company store.

There was no union and most of the time John was paid less than a dollar for every ton of coal he shoveled in a 12-hour day. Most days with a pick and shovel he could load six or seven tons of coal unless he was working a vein of hard coal that was stubborn to budge or a narrow vein that required him to lie on his back or side; then he might manage to load only four or five tons of coal in a day.

When Rhoda was 17, their first child, Jerry Wayne, was born; at 24, Robert Jay; at 26, General Grant, who was nicknamed "Did"; at 28, Noah Sam; at 31, June Katherine; at 39, Mary Ruth. Finally at 43, their last child, Mattie Lee, was born.

From the time Rhoda was old enough to know what a bible was, she found herself drawn to the ways of the Holy Spirit. In fact, those who knew her agreed that Rhoda's religious life was the most important thing in the whole world to her. The Smith family was fairly religious but the sibling she felt closest to, her sister Mary, was the most prone to feel the strong pull of the spiritual world.

After the birth of their first child Jerry Wayne, Rhoda was busy but gradually became bored and disillusioned. Marriage was not the enjoyable union she had anticipated. In their rural area, their only social outlet was going to the small Pentecostal church nearby twice a week and joining a few neighborhood ladies for bible study. She remained steadfast in her prayer and church attendance. In the small church she relished the shouts of "Amen!" and "Thank you, Jesus", the feeling of camaraderie and the promise of a joyous and heavenly future that would be recompense for the suffering and disappointment of her earthly life.

John was a good and honest man but he didn't share her predilection for religion. She saw the hand of God in every human experience and every natural event. He did not. He saw humans and the world they inhabited as natural, rather than divine, creations. He saw no evidence that God intervened in human affairs; instead, he believed that humans were on their own. Those who got to know him well said he had become cynical because of the hardships and inequalities he had experienced.

Although he rarely pondered religious matters, he tried to be patient and supportive of his wife's beliefs. But he considered many Christians to be hypocritical and delusional, even deceitful. Besides that, he was a quiet soul and somewhat of a loner. The shouting and other histrionics of those who were moved by the Spirit made him uncomfortable.

Rhoda didn't like the fact that they didn't see eye to eye on religion, but she realized that life was hard for him and that some of his experiences, like losing his mother at a young age, had made him bitter.

As a young girl, Rhoda had discovered the rush of excitement and sense of freedom she felt when she attended a tent revival in the area. But as a wife and mother, she felt trapped and stifled at home. They didn't have a phone and, except for church, her only social contacts were a few neighbors within walking distance. When her boys were old enough to occupy themselves, she started attending revivals again.

She liked the attention she didn't always get at home and the compliments the preacher paid her. And, after all, wasn't she doing the Lord's work? She felt called to a work more important than anything else—more important even than home or family. In Matthew 19:29, didn't Jesus say that everyone who leaves his home or family for His sake will receive a hundred times more and inherit eternal life?

Rhoda was envious of her sister Mary because she had money and seemed to live a more carefree and exciting life. Rhoda never learned to drive. At first, she could only attend church services and revivals that were held close by on Sunday mornings or Wednesday evenings. Besides she couldn't depend on John to transport her to church on any day but Sunday and even a Sunday was sometimes a challenge. He often worked on Saturdays and was worn out by Sunday.

But Mary could drive. And Mary had enough money to finance short outings. She was also chafing at the constraints of marriage and eager to renew her church involvement. Rhoda and Mary started going to revivals together.

Rhoda wanted to work and bring home some extra money, but there were few jobs for women in Harlan County, except as school teachers or secretaries, and she didn't have enough education for those jobs. She was forced to take small jobs such as washing clothes and cleaning for other families who could afford to pay for help.

Although John didn't want her to take a job, he finally acquiesced because their dire financial condition left them no other choice. He felt inadequate and a failure because he couldn't support his family.

By the time their oldest daughter June was ten years old and able to cook and clean, Rhoda loaned her to Uncle Will Smith whose wife was blind and to Mary's family to make a little extra money. After June had left home when her sister Ruth was about ten years old, Rhoda sent Ruth to help with chores at Uncle Will's In her place.

When Rhoda returned from one of her longer absences at revivals some distance from home, she found her two youngest daughters in a sorry state. She realized something had to be done. After praying about it, she decided the Lord wanted her to quit doing laundry for other people and get a real job.

After mining, the railroad was the second biggest employer in Harlan County so she talked herself into a job with Louisville & Nashville Railroad. She cooked for the employees on a train that traveled the rails through eastern Kentucky into eastern Tennessee. She was gone a week at a time but she took her youngest daughter Mattie Lee with her.

Pentecostals interpret the bible literally. They don't believe in doctors; they dance and shout when the Holy Spirit descends upon them; and some purport to speak in unknown tongues, what others call gibberish. In some Pentecostal churches, as signs of faith and salvation, members are even encouraged to handle poisonous snakes, drink poison and walk on, or handle, red hot coals. It should be pointed out, however, that women seem more restrained in their professions of faith and tend to leave these kinds of behaviors to the men.

Mark 16:17-18 in the 1611 King James version of scripture reads:

"And these signs shall follow them that believe: In my name shall they cast out devils; they shall speak with new tongues; they shall take up serpents; and if they drink any deadly thing, it shall not hurt them; they shall lay hands on the sick, and they shall recover."

In one of Rhoda's early experiences at a Sunday service in the small Holiness Church near their log home, the congregation was aroused by the preacher's fervent sermon and exhortations to prove their faith. Several members were overcome by the Holy Spirit and began shouting expressions of their faith. Some of the members spoke loudly in unknown tongues and danced around in their pews.

Suddenly, overcome by the Holy Spirit, an older man named Bob dashed to the small wood burning stove, spit in his hands and threw open the door. He snatched out a red hot coal, juggled it in his hands and quickly passed it on to a young man named Cooper who was standing beside him. Without thinking Cooper juggled it briefly and tossed it to a surprised middle aged man named Paul.

Rhoda and a young man named Carlo had approached to watch the spectacle. Too close: before she knew it, the preacher had rushed up behind her in his eagerness to take charge and bumped into her, causing her to stumble forward into the *line of fire*.

Her eyes grew wide in panic; the wild-eyed Paul, desperately juggling the hot coal, saw her as his salvation. She threw up her hands in defense and jumped aside. "*Sheemi ma sharlow*, give it to Carlo!" she shouted and pointed at him as she hastily backed away.

But Carlo would have none of that. "Nooo," he shouted while flailing his arms to push onlookers out of the way and fled from the church. That was the last they saw of him. Or Paul.

From then on, Rhoda was often moved to speak in tongues and she did so with great pride. She never figured out where those strange words came from, but she did learn to stay in the back when things got wild and to leave it to the men to handle the snakes and pass around the hot coals.

As adults her three daughters often recalled that little story about their mother speaking in unknown tongues and chuckled about it. Perhaps not surprisingly, her three daughters never felt the desire to be churchgoers. That might be in part because Rhoda didn't hesitate to flail her girls severely when they stepped out of line. She fully embraced Proverbs verse 13:24 that reads: "Whoever spares the rod hates their children, but the one who loves their children is careful to discipline them."

Those were hard times during the depression years, especially for June and Ruth who were sometimes left on their own for weeks at a time. Being older, their brothers were gone most of the time, free to roam around the country unsupervised. Their father was working long days at the mines and unable to look after them so they missed a lot of school and often went hungry. Ironically it was a repeat of the life he had lived as a child.

One day when they were left alone, they were hungry and desperate. June had a bright idea. She had noticed small fish—minnows and sunfish—swimming in the shallow stream near their log cabin. They grabbed an old bucket and rushed to the stream where they eventually caught two small fish, about as long as their small hands. They had to figure out how to cook them but there was no cooking oil or lard in the kitchen. They tried to heat them on the warm stones of the fireplace but they weren't hot enough so they still went hungry.

Sometime around 1935, Rhoda and Mary heard of a remarkable young woman named Effie Gilmer who lived in southwestern Virginia not far from where Mary lived. She had a flourishing ministry in the Holiness or Pentecostal Church tradition.

Effie Gilmer preached all over Southern Virginia in tent revivals. She was charismatic with piercing eyes that seemed to look right into the soul. Many believed she could heal the sick. She wore long dresses and had her hair cut short. She had a clear and beautiful voice, preached powerful sermons and appealed especially to women. Rhoda and Mary were infatuated and decided they had to meet her.

Mary heard about a revival that was going to be held by Effie near Middlesboro, Kentucky on a Saturday afternoon. She got all excited and talked Rhoda into going with her. Mary drove to Harlan and picked up Rhoda for the 40 mile trip to Middlesboro. Although June was only twelve years old and Ruth was barely five—this was before Mattie was born—Rhoda thought it would be okay to leave Ruth in June's care.

When they heard Effie Gilmer preach, they were overcome with excitement. It was as if Effie was talking directly to them, understanding the trials and tribulations they endured as women, encouraging them to put their faith in Jesus to solve their problems. She preached that they should even leave their husbands and families if they were not happy and felt called to do so.

From then on, Mary and Rhoda kept up with Effie's revivals and went to them as often as they could get away. Sometimes Mary would come by late at night and Rhoda would sneak away with her for a couple of days. Eventually, their outings grew into weeks at a time when her young daughters had to fend for themselves while their father worked long days in the mines.

Sometimes this infuriated John and drove him to despair because of his concern for the girls. Nevertheless, at early ages June and Ruth were independent and self-reliant, brave enough to leave home and tough enough to make it on their own while they were still teenagers. They learned to think for themselves. Although their mother was a zealous Christian, the brand of religion she practiced did not sit well with her three daughters because it seemed harsh and unforgiving.

They learned three important lessons: first, they had to fend for themselves because there was nobody they could depend on to look after them, and nobody seemed to care about them anyway, except for their brothers Sam and "Did"; second, they had to get the hell out of Harlan; and, third, the only way they were going to make it in a man's world was to be tough and never give up no matter how hard they were slapped down.

Rhoda Brittian in her later years

June

June Katherine Brittian was born to John and Rhoda Brittian on February 18, 1925 in Pennington Gap, Virginia. It was a bitterly cold Wednesday with shifting drifts of snow. Pennington Gap was a small farming community of maybe a thousand souls in rural Lee County where the southwestern tip of Virginia meets Kentucky and Tennessee. The vast majority of the men folk in Lee County worked either in farming—with tobacco being the main cash crop—or coal mining. The majority of the women folk there were home makers.

June was the first girl, after four boys, to be born to Rhoda. When she was six years old, June was hit by a car. She ran out into the road while walking with her father. The doctors said she would be crippled for the rest of her life. But within a year, she did walk again, although she carried a jagged scar on her leg from the accident for the rest of her life.

Even as a child she was strong-willed and defiant. She learned at a tender age to make do on her own. Since her parents were not available most of the time, June learned early on that she couldn't depend on other people, even her parents. She became tough and independent and she learned not to trust anyone who wasn't family and even some who were family.

Her father worked the coal mines six days a week. The job was backbreaking and left him depleted and resigned to a life that felt desperate and hopeless. There were always worries about whether or not he would earn enough money to put groceries on the table. He was never harsh with any of his children but he didn't have the time or the strength to nurture or love them.

John was forced to leave most of the parenting up to Rhoda, but she seemed to be more concerned with spiritual matters than with being a mother to their children.

June had a painfully limited childhood with few playmates since they lived in a rural area with no close neighbors. She had four older brothers but her three older brothers were five to 14 years older than she was so she didn't get to spend much time with them. Sam, her youngest brother, was only three years older than she, but their interests were so different they didn't spend a lot of time together. Sam did protect June from bullies at school so he was much beloved by her.

June's childhood was not a happy one. She had no way to get around and, for girls, there were few places to go to anyway. The only place she could go to meet other children her age was at the small nearby Pentecostal church she sometimes attended with her mother.

By the time June was eight years old, she had learned how to cook and clean house. Rhoda sometimes sent her out to cook and clean house for other families in the neighborhood. Rhoda even sent her to help her Aunt Mary in Pennington Gap for weeks at a time.

Her mother was religious but harsh and cold toward her. When she was about eight years old, her mother hit her so hard with a stick of firewood that the splinter left a large scar on her leg for the rest of her life.

The Brittian home was a chaotic place. There was considerable fighting among the boys but June learned how to hold her own with them. Her brother Jay was a bully; sometimes he would take the food their mother had cooked and not allow anyone else to eat until he had eaten all he wanted. It didn't matter to him if there was nothing left for the rest of the family. He didn't hesitate to slap his mother's face if he didn't like what she wanted him to do. He would even threaten his father who was unable to make him mind.

In 1937 when June was 12, she quit school. She was sick of being made fun of. She couldn't remember going to school with clothes as nice as those most of the other kids wore. Her wardrobe consisted of hand-me-downs and dresses and underwear sewn from flour sacks.

America had landed smack-dab in the midst of the Great Depression and times were hard for most everybody in the country but they were brutally hard on the Brittians and the other families in Harlan County. In 1939, almost ten years after the Great Depression began, the unemployment rate remained over 20 per cent.

Her father was still a coal miner and, although the four boys had moved out, he still struggled to support his wife and daughters. Every day June saw her parents scrabbling to make ends meet.

Another reason she quit school was that neither of her parents seemed to care whether she and her little sister Ruth went to school or not. Truth of the matter was, both of her parents were too beaten down to care much about anything but scraping out a living. Rhoda believed that the only hope for either of her daughters was to find a good man and marry him.

June believed that as well but she never met any good men. If they had a job, most of the men in Harlan County worked in the mines and she swore she wasn't going to wind up like her mother. She watched her mother growing old with nothing to look forward to except going to church year after year. Nothing ever changed.

Rhoda had come from a fairly well off family with high expectations that she would marry well and live a good life. Why shouldn't her life be a comfortable one without hardship? Her mother had tried to talk her out of marrying John, but he was handsome and she was young and impressionable.

By the time June was 16, her breasts were well developed and she was maturing and attractive. Her sex drive was revving up and she craved male companionship. Besides that, she was willing to do anything to leave home. It was her way of rebelling against her mother's harshness and the hard life that she knew awaited her if she didn't leave Harlan County.

That was in early 1942; America had entered World War II and most of the young men who would have found her attractive had left Harlan County to join the Army or Navy. Her mother took her to church where a few scrawny teenage boys caught her eye, but, upon getting to know them, she found them juvenile and unattractive. She lost interest quickly and ignored them. She often complained to her handful of girlfriends that every damn fellow she met was either too young or too old for her.

Like other large coal companies, Kits Mining had its own store. The company store was not just the local grocery store but usually the center of life in a coal mining town. Every company town had one, and every miner's family shopped there. The company store was usually located near the railroad tracks in the town. Everything that a family might want or need could be bought in the store, from food to clothing, from hardware supplies and the miners' tools to furniture and appliances.

The company store served other functions besides being a grocery store. It was the one place where neighbors and friends could came together without the formal organization of church or lodge or school. It was the community bank and bulletin board, a place where housewives gathered to discuss meals, children, and neighborhood gossip. Offices of company management were usually located in the company store, as was the U. S. Post Office serving that community. Records for everything to do with the miners were kept there: a miner's time sheets; number of cars loaded that week; rent, light and coal deductions; doctor's fees and script[1] advances. Often the payroll window was set up in the store, so that miners gathered there on Friday afternoons to collect their pay.

One day when June was 17, her mother caught a ride to the company store and took June with her. June couldn't help but notice the handsome young man with sandy hair behind the counter.

Blue-eyed, clean-shaven and well-dressed, he was the bookkeeper for the store. When he spoke, she could tell he was educated. He couldn't help but notice the attractive young girl in the plain dress.

She was an attractive brunet with big brown eyes and a seductive smile. While her mother was busy placing her order, he asked June her name and she told him. His name was James Gordon and he was the

---

[1] "Script" - an advance against unearned wages issued by a coal company in lieu of cash to its miners for redeemption only at the company store—often in the form of coupon books or round metal tokens.

company's bookkeeper. He was 24, a suitable age, and there was no ring on his finger.

From then on June accompanied her mother to the company store every chance she got. Her mother wasn't fooled; she could tell June had a crush on the young man who was considerably older than her daughter. She believed that James was too uppity to be attracted to a girl from a poor family like theirs.

But June had other ideas. Her parents didn't have a telephone so the only way she could communicate with James when she wasn't with her mother was by smuggling a note to him. With a little persuading, her friend Lily Darby agreed to help her. Lily's brother Joshua worked at a hardware store delivering supplies. From time to time he delivered tools and parts to the Kits Mining Company in Alva where James and June's father worked. Sometimes Josh was able to carry a note to James when he was making a delivery to the mining company.

Jim Gordon had a car—a black 1939 two-door Dodge Coup with white walls. That was a big deal. When a young man in his 20s drove a nice car like that, he pretty much had his pick of the ladies. One day in May Josh dropped by the company store and gave Jim a note that June had scribbled out.

Jim read her note and hastily sent a reply in which he asked her if he could pick her up on Saturday and take her to a burger joint in Harlan. The possibility of going on a date with him—her first date ever—launched her into a state of euphoria.

Her mother was in the kitchen. "Mommy, Jim Gordon has asked me out on a date. He wants to take me to Harlan to get something to eat."

Rhoda stopped and placed her hands on her hips and frowned. "June, you're not old enough to go on a date with that man."

"I'm seventeen years old and he's got a car and a good job. Besides I like him a lot. Can I go with him, please?"

Rhoda put her hand on her forehead and thought for a minute. Then she narrowed her eyes. "All right, June, go on, but do not hold hands with that man. Do not kiss him and do not hug him. I don't trust him."

June hugged her mother. "I won't, Mommy, I promise."

She ran over to the Darby house as soon as she could, dying to tell Lily about her date. It was the most exciting thing that had ever happened to her. She knocked on the front door of the Darby's house and hollered for Lily.

Lily had never seen such a wide grin on her. "What's gotten into you?" She said.

She spouted it out, "I've got a date with Jim." She gripped Lily's hand, "Come on, let's go for a walk."

"Jim Gordon! Why I do declare. I want to hear all about it," Lily giggled.

"He's going to pick me up and take me to Harlan to get something to eat. The only thing is I'm scared to death. I've never been on a date before. I don't know what to do."

Lily laughed. "Don't worry about it. Just be yourself, get to know him. You know, ask him a lot of questions, make him feel important."

June looked puzzled. "Umm, you mean relax?"

"Yes, Silly. Just relax." The depth of June's innocence suddenly dawned on Lily; she became concerned. "June, has your mother ever talked to you about sex?"

"Sex—are you crazy!" She rolled her eyes. "If I ever uttered the word *sex*, my mother would whip me within an inch of my life. My mother would never talk about sex. She did warn me that I would go straight to hell if I ever had sex with a man I wasn't married to. The only advice I ever got from her was to keep my knees together anytime I'm with a man. And no huggin', kissin' or hand holdin' until there's a ring on my finger."

Lily regarded June sternly and wagged her finger: "Well, I'm gonna' warn you: you can't trust a man, none of 'em. Men aren't like women, June. There's one thing on their mind."

"You mean sex?"

"Yes ma'am. They'll pretend they love you—or sometimes they just think they do." She paused for effect. "But all they really have on their mind is Sex and they'll tell you anything to get their way with you."

"But I really like Jim; I want to have sex with him. I get so excited when I see him I can't stand it. I know we're supposed to wait 'til we're married but . . ."

Lily grabbed her by the shoulders and shook her. "June, for God's sake, you don't even know him. Have you forgot what happened to me? I thought Virgil loved me, but when I got pregnant I like to never got that son-uhva-bitch to marry me. Then after I had Mitch, he lost interest and decided he didn't want to be married. He dumped me and moved to Ohio. That's why I'm gonna' be living with Momma and Daddy until the day I die."

"Aw, Lil', I'm sorry." She brightened up and hugged her friend tightly. "Hey, you're awful pretty, Lil'. You'll meet a good man and . . ."

"No, I won't. Men don't want to marry a woman with a baby. Besides, how can I ever meet anybody? There ain't nothin' here but the dregs of manhood."

"Maybe the war will be over soon, Lil'. Then you'll have your pick of the fellows coming back from the war."

I sure hope so, Lily thought. "I sure hope you're right, June, but I've been slapped down so many times I'm afraid to get my hopes up."

When James Gordon came calling at the Brittian log cabin, June was all dolled up. She had talked her mother into fixing her hair up real nice and she and her mother had found a dress at a used clothing store that looked good on her.

James came in and briefly chatted with June's mother and father. June was nervous, and so was James, but not so much. No one knew quite what to say so the conversation between the four of them was stiff and clumsy. When they were alone, however, June followed Lilly's advice and to her surprise they found each other easy to talk to.

After their date, June breathlessly declared to Lily that it was the best time she had ever had. James Gordon was too good to be true. Before long she was professing her love for him to Lily. Sometimes she fantasized about marrying him and moving to Harlan where his parents lived or to the big city of Williamsburg.

Lily would always smile and wish her friend the best, but deep down inside she was uneasy. At night when no one else was around, she would whisper to herself, *Dear Lord, don't let June end up like me. Please, Lord, not like me.*

Christmas Carols & Flour Sacks

C hristmas eve 1933. Harlan, Kentucky. It was a dreary day slipping into twilight with a bone-chilling wind that laid a dusting of snow on the ground. There was a pine wreath with holly berries on the front door of the old log cabin for decoration and a lighted candle in the window.

John Brittian slumped over the small kitchen table with his elbows on the table and his head in his hands as Rhoda finished cooking the Christmas meal. From time to time he leaned back in his chair and sighed, trying to follow Rhoda's prattle about the local gossip and the world going to hell and appear interested. The only light in the kitchen came from the kerosene lamp on the table; the old cook stove in the kitchen provided its only warmth.

The whole family was not often together but, on Christmas or Thanksgiving holidays, Rhoda insisted that the family stay home for the family meal.

That evening she would attend a candle light service at the small Pentecostal church near by. She was looking forward to the Christmas service and seeing some of their neighbors. She had implored John to attend the service with her and he eventually gave in. But she could tell his heart was not in it and she resigned herself to the fact that he would probably back out.

He sometimes grumbled that the church goers there were too serious and the sermons depressing—life was hard enough, he said, without a vengeful God watching your every move and making you feel guilty. And why in God's name would anyone in their right mind want to handle poisonous snakes?

To him that simple act of defiance was one of the few ways he could cope with a life over which he had little control. Being out of work and having no money made him feel trapped and powerless. The only way he could conjure up any sense of self-worth was to stand his ground and declare to his wife and to God: "I will not go!" He found God easier to stand up to than his wife: sometimes he was still forced to give in to her to keep the peace.

To her it was a battle she could not win because of his stubbornness. Once more she fretted about the poor example he set, making it hard to get her sons to go to church with her. "If you don't go to church, the Devil will get you!" she sternly warned them repeatedly but, for some reason she could never fathom, they remained unmoved.

One by one, as their sons arrived and showered affection on their dejected parents, John and Rhoda's spirits lifted and they put aside their resentments and frustrations with each other. After all, it was Christmas!

Rhoda had been busy that afternoon cooking dinner on their old wood stove: cathead biscuits and gravy, fried apples and turnip greens. There was no roasted turkey, no fried chicken, not even stewed rabbit or squirrel. After making her biscuits, the flour hopper in the kitchen cabinet was empty.

June set the table and laid two sprigs of holly by the kerosene lamp. Then she fixed a cup of hot chocolate for herself and her brothers. The only other festive part of the meal would be a Payday candy bar for each of the boys and June and a bag of peanuts to be shared. There would be no presents.

June was almost nine years old, big enough to help her mother with the cooking and to entertain Ruth, the youngest member of the family, who was barely 18 months old. June was fascinated by her little sister and loved babysitting her.

June loved her big brothers, too. She was happy when they were around and they paid attention to her. All four of them were there, gathered around the small fireplace in the front room. Jerry was 22; he realized his parents were under great stress and agonized over how he might help them. Jay, who was almost 16 and the most rowdy, bantered with "Did", age 13, who seemed to be lost in thought. Sam, age 11, couldn't be still because he was desperately hungry. There was not a lot to be happy about.

Most days in the summer there was enough to eat. The children picked blackberries, muscadines and mulberries, gathered walnuts, persimmons and paw paws, and foraged for mushrooms and poke salad whenever it was in season. And the Brittians usually had a small garden.

But winters were tough; the family had to depend on canned fruits and vegetables and staples like dried pinto beans.

They were in the midst of the Great Depression, and unemployment had reached 25% in many places, but it was even worse in the coal mining country of eastern Kentucky and in other southern states such as Alabama. Between 1930 and 1933, more than 9,000 banks closed in the U.S., taking with them millions of people's savings.

John had been dreading the approach of Christmas because their meager savings were gone and he had no money to spend on Christmas presents or a Christmas dinner for his wife and children. The icebox was nearly empty and there was no credit remaining on his account at the company store. The soles of his sons' shoes were thin as cardboard and June's dresses were stitched together from flour sacks.

He tried to sound cheerful and even joked a little with the boys, but the fact that he had not worked since early December weighed heavily on his mind. He had no idea how they would make it to the end of January without starving if he wasn't called back to work soon. He was deeply worried but he kept his worries to himself and determined to push them out of his mind for the rest of the evening.

The only source of entertainment for the family was the old Zenith tube radio John had bought for $39 on installments the previous summer. John and Rhoda listened to the news, and she enjoyed programs of preaching and gospel singing.

The bright spot during the Christmas holidays was always the Christmas carols. They were broadcast on radio station WOPI out of Bristol. That small AM radio station, the first one from Knoxville to Roanoke, began broadcasting in 1929. Even though the signal was often weak and staticky, the whole family loved to gather around and listen to Christmas carols on WOPI.

Some days during the Christmas season, if the weather wasn't too bad, a small group of carolers from the Baptist Church would make the rounds in their neighborhood singing Christmas carols, laughing and renewing friendships. Those were the days when the world seemed at peace and people were happy, no matter how poor they were. Those were special times when John and Rhoda cast aside their troubles, gave in to the magic of Christmas and felt their love for each other renewed.

Times were lean for most people during the Great Depression. Scrimping and saving by reusing everything possible became a way of life. Younger children "made do" with hand-me-downs that were "recycled" from their older siblings.

Few rural families had enough money to buy new clothes at a store, so mothers mended socks and sewed patches over the holes in their clothes. Back then ladies liked to sew, so a lot of the clothes were homemade.

Amidst widespread poverty in the '30s, thrifty women in Appalachia noticed that their flour and livestock feed came in large cloth sacks. Farm women began to use the sacks as fabric to sew everything from girls' dresses and blouses to boys' shirts and even underpants. When the clothing finally wore out, it would be cut up and made into something else, like a quilt or dishtowel.

Some women even used their sewing skills to bring in some extra cash, sewing dresses and other items for friends and neighbors. Rhoda was no exception. Because she didn't have much money to spend on clothing, she became a skilled seamstress using recycled flour sacks.

When June attended the elementary school at Verne, some of the other children regularly made fun of her because of her ill-fitting, homemade clothes. Her teacher knew about the hurtful teasing but did nothing to stop it. As a result, June began to hate going to school.

When she was in the third grade, she usually walked to school with her older brother Sam. One day she seemed especially downcast, so he asked her why she hated going to school so much. When she confessed that a couple of the boys were bullying and making fun of her in front of her friends because of the clothes she wore, he stopped in his tracks, bent over and looked her in the eye.

"It's Charles and Eddy, ain't it?"

With her eyes cast down, she nodded yes.

Sam adored his little sister and he wasn't going to allow anyone to pick on her. He stood up and clinched his fist. Then he relaxed. "Don't worry, Sis', I'll take care of that," he smiled. Then he hugged her.

She had on one of her older flour sack dresses and a well-worn pair of panties with a loose-fitting waist band. When recess came, the children were sent out into the yard for an hour of play time. Several of her classmates wanted to play dodge ball and they invited June to play. They liked her because she was agile and moved quickly. She wanted to play too but she hesitated because her clothes were loose fitting. Finally she gave in to the dares and started to play.

When Charles and Eddy saw her, they insisted on joining in. When Charles threw the ball hard at her, she jumped aside so quickly that her panties fell down around her feet. The two boys laughed at her and cruelly made fun of her in front of her classmates. Embarrassed and ashamed, she ran behind the school house and began to cry.

One of the girls ran to tell June's brother. When Sam heard what had happened, he roared, "Where are they!" When he caught up with Charles, Sam grabbed him by the collar, spun him around and gave him a black eye and a bloody nose. When Eddy saw Sam coming for him with a look on his face that registered *I'm going to plant you in the mud*, Eddy almost wet his pants trying to get away. Sam scared those two boys so badly they were on their best behavior from then on if they were around June. It was the last time she was ever bothered by bullies.

After the onset of World War II, things changed. Cotton had to be rationed to make uniforms for the military, so manufacturers had to give up their fabric in order to support the war effort. After the war, cheaper paper sacks became available, so the usual colorful and sturdy fabrics gradually disappeared. From then on, flour was packaged in paper bags and flour sack clothes were soon forgotten.

Little Chickens

Harvey Perkins felt his age as he rubbed the sleep from his eyes and made a strong pot of coffee. His wife Hattie was away visiting her mother in Williamsburg. From his small kitchen window he caught a glimpse of two small, skinny girls as they warily approached his chicken coop. He had an aging rooster he called "Rufus" and six hens that supplied him and his wife with more than enough eggs. It wasn't unusual to see some of the neighborhood kids hanging around his chicken coop because young children were drawn to his chickens and loved to feed his goat.

As he looked more closely, he recognized the two frail and bashful Brittian girls; June, the older of the two, was about twelve and Ruth, her little sister, was no more than five years old.

He sighed and shook his head. Rhoda must be away again, he thought, leaving the girls to fend for themselves while John works in the mines.

Sometimes the girls were left on their own for weeks at a time. Mattie Lee, the youngest of the three girls, was not with her sisters so Perkins assumed she must be with her mother . . . somewhere.

Since the Brittians lived only a few houses away, he knew the family fairly well. John Brittian was a serious but likable man and a hard worker but his family of nine was desperately poor. Although he put in long hours, he was paid so little that he struggled to support his family. He was a miner at the Kits mines where he worked six days a week from

7:00 am to 7:00 pm and was paid 75 cents for every ton of coal he loaded.

Anyone could tell from the rough and ill-fitting clothes the Brittians wore and their lean and hungry look that they were a family barely managing to survive during the hard times of the '30's. Times were tough all over the country, but they were especially hard in the coal mining towns of eastern Kentucky. It was a ruggedly mountainous land, unsuitable for farming, with little industry and few jobs in anything but mining.

Perkins had worked for the L&N railroad for 28 years and received a small pension. Over the years, he had even managed to save almost $10,000. He felt sorry for the Brittian family because he knew that John Brittian had no pension, no benefits and not a penny of savings.

Perkins often saw John on Sundays working with one or two of his sons, doing chores around their small clapboard house. There was a garden behind the house where his oldest son Jerry was charged with raising a few vegetables to help feed the family with fresh produce during the summer months and canned goods during the cold months.

Perkins was lost in thought when the motion caught his eye and he noticed June lift up a corner of the chicken wire just enough so that Ruth could shimmy through. June looked around apprehensively as her sister scurried to a nest and picked up three eggs. Then June motioned for her to hurry back through the opening.

"Why them little scallywags!" Perkins snorted as he started for the door to yell at them.

But they were running as fast as their little legs would carry them, their unkempt hair streaming behind them. They were so thin and he could tell they were scared. He stopped, unable to scold them. *Good for you, girls*, he thought. He sunk down in the old wooden chair on the porch. *I'd better not tell Hattie who's been stealin' our eggs*, he mused. *She'll insist that I complain to John and they'll get whuped.*

He knew their father wouldn't whup them, but their mother would sure 'nuff beat the tar out of them when she returned. He closed his eyes and rubbed his chin. *I can't have that*, he thought, *they're starving to death*. As he gazed out at his chicken coop, he began to smile. *I could fix that loose chicken wire but, nah, I don't think I will; my back's actin' up.*

The next morning, as John Brittian left the house to catch his ride to the mine, he spotted a little basket on his porch with six eggs in it. He glanced toward the Perkins house and thought, *Thanks, Harvey*!

After Hattie returned from her visit and took up cooking again, she noticed there weren't many eggs in the ice box. "Harvey, how many eggs did you eat while I was gone? I barely have enough to make a skillet of cornbread!"

Harvey took a deep breath. "Uhh, . . . well, come to think of it, I guess I have eaten a few of them. You know it's easy to cook an egg."

She ignored her husband: "Hmmm, I swear, Harvey, I think somebody's stealing our eggs."

He swallowed hard and managed a grin. "Maybe ol' Rufus is like me—too old to strut his stuff anymore."

"Huhh," Hattie huffed. "If he is, we'll get us a young rooster and have Rufus for Sunday dinner."

"Aww, it's probably that possum I saw prowlin' 'round." Harvey feigned a concerned look. "I'll watch for it. Why, I'll fetch my shotgun and we'll have him for Sunday dinner."

Hattie rolled her eyes. "If you shoot that possum, don't you dare bring that thing in my kitchen."

Two days later, early one morning as Hattie Perkins was making sausage gravy and biscuits for breakfast, she glanced out the window and saw two little girls sneaking up to the chicken coop. The taller of the two girls looked around cautiously and pulled up a corner of the chicken wire as the smaller one scrambled through the opening. Before the smaller one could grab any eggs, Hattie charged outside toward the chicken coop, fuming. "I knew it! I knew it! You're the ones stealin' my eggs!" she yelled. June looked up, terrified at the large red faced woman rushing toward her.

"No, Ma'am," June stammered. "We was just trying to get our cat."

"Don't you lie to me," Hattie screeched. "There ain't no cat in there!"

Ruth scrambled through the hole in the chicken wire and the two of them took off like a shot.

"Harvey! Them Brittian girls was sneakin' into our coop. Said they was chasin' their cat. Huhh!"

Harvey gingerly stepped down off the porch and ambled toward his wife. "Oh, I'm sure they were, Dear."

"Well, I doubt that," she grumbled.

He put his arm around her shoulder. "Aw, they're just kids, Hattie. No harm done."

"They're stealin' our eggs, Harvey. Don't you think you oughta do somethin' 'bout it?"

Harvey looked concerned. "I reckon I should. Now don't you fret, Hattie. I'll take care of it."

Suddenly he put his nose in the air and turned toward the house. "Say, that's not the biscuits I smell burnin', is it?"

"Oh, my heavens," she gasped and rushed back toward the house.

A Predicament

O ne Saturday morning in early August of 1943, June woke up feeling out of sorts. Her period was a week late and she was starting to worry. At first she hadn't thought much about it; maybe she had miscounted. She counted the days again–twice; no, she had not! She teared up as she went outside and sat on the porch, uneasily mulling over her predicament. *What if I'm pregnant? What would Jim think about that?* she fretted. *And what would Mommy do? Probably run me off.* Her thoughts frightened her. She couldn't decide which would be worse—Jim's reaction or her mother's.

The silly cackling of two guineas wandering into the yard caught her attention. She wiped her eyes and smiled at the two odd birds, bantering back and forth like an old married couple, and managed to briefly push the thought of being pregnant out of her mind. She decided to wait one more day to see if she got her period.

Two weeks later June was still waiting and she was panicking. She and Jim had dated for about four months. Yes, they had experienced mystically glorious sex three times in the cramped front seat of his '39 Dodge Coupe. It occurred to her that maybe the next time she saw him she should casually say, *"By the way, 'Jimmy Boy', my period is three weeks late. I think I'm pregnant with your baby! What do you think of that?"*

On second thought, she decided: *no, not yet.*

To make matters worse, she hadn't seen Jim or heard from him in several weeks and she was beginning to suspect he was seeing someone else. It was maddening. Her family had no phone so there was no way to talk to him unless she caught a ride with a neighbor to the company store where he worked. Her older brothers were all away fighting in WWII so they couldn't help. Besides that, her parents traded at the company store on the weekend when Jim wasn't working so it usually did no good to ride with them.

As the days dragged by, she became ever more anxious. Every now and then she would catch her mother looking at her with a troubled look on her face. Did her mother suspect that she was hiding something? Or was she just feeling guilty and imagining that her mother knew her secret? Maybe her mother had noticed that her underwear had not been soiled by the blood from her period in a long time.

June remembered what her mother always said when she heard some girl had gotten pregnant out of wedlock: "It's a disgrace . . and a sin!" she would declare. "I would disown a daughter of mine who let that happen."

Four weeks after her period was due, she was desperate, bustin' to talk to somebody, anybody besides her mother who would only yell at her and slap her around at just the thought of getting pregnant before getting married. She decided to make the 2.5 mile walk along the small river called Martins Fork to see Mary Lou Sinclair who had become a mother nearly a year earlier. She was one of the handful of friends June had managed to stay in touch with after quitting elementary school.

Mary Lou was sitting on the porch in a rickety old rocking chair with her baby asleep in blankets beside her when she saw June laboring up the hill, breathing hard. Mary Lou scrambled to her feet and ran to meet her friend. After giving June a mighty hug, she whooped, "Lord have mercy, if you ain't a sight for sore eyes! What on earth brings you up here, June?"

"I came here to see you, Lou. It's been too long since I've seen you and I need to talk to somebody, uhh, somebody I can trust . . ."

Mary Lou studied June's face intently, becoming concerned. She took June by the hand and walked her up to the porch. "About what, June? Are you in trouble?"

"Uhh, no," June blushed and then stammered, "Well, yes, I guess I am."

She lowered her voice, "I think I'm pregnant."

"Pregnant!"

"Yes, I'm four weeks past due and . . ."

"Have you ever been that late before?" Mary Lou interrupted.

"No."

They sat down on the steps and lowered their voices to keep from waking the baby.

"Did he use a rubber?"

"No."

Mary Lou frowned: "Oh. Well, have you felt sick in the morning lately?"

"Uhh, yeah. Day before yesterday. I felt like I was gonna' throw up."

Mary Lou gasped: "Oh, my Lord, child, you are pregnant."

June stared at the ground and pursed her lips. "Damn it. I was afraid of that. I kept hopin' it wasn't so. Now I don't know what to do; I reckon Mommy will run me off for sure when I tell her."

"Your daddy wouldn't let her do that, would he?" Mary Lou gasped.

"I don't know, Lou. He has a hard time with her. When it comes to gettin' her way; she's awful stubborn. Even if he didn't let her run me off, she would make it hard on me—I couldn't stay there. I couldn't bear the way she would treat me."

"What about your man, June? Has he told you he loves you? He'll stay with you . . . and stand up for you, won't he?"

"I don't know, Lou. He never said he loved me. I just don't know. I ain't seen him in a month. I didn't want to say anything about it until I was sure." She looked down at the ground and choked back tears. "Truth is, I'm afraid he may be seeing somebody else."

"Oh, for the love of God! That's not right." She shook her head in disgust. I despise the way men are . . . They've got one thing on their mind and when they get what they want, they drop you. The selfish bastards! They're never satisfied. They just use women, especially poor women like us."

"Well, I've got to find a way to see Jim and find out what he aims to do about me being pregnant."

Mary Lou curled her lip in disgust. "Damn it! Waitin' is all we do. It's like we're just sittin' around in a bus station, waitin' for some guy to notice us and take us somewhere. Meanwhile, they're getting on with their lives, doin' as they please. Damn it! It ain't fair."

"Yeah, I know. But what the shit can I do except wait for him to make the first move?"

"Look here, June, if he does get it in his mind to leave you high and dry, you know what I would do if I was you . . ." She clenched her teeth and spit out the words: "I would tell your parents he raped you. Or even better, if your brothers could get their hands on him, I bet he would change his mind real fast about not wantin' to get married."

"Sure, Jay or Jerry could teach him a lesson. Trouble is, my brothers are still fightin' overseas. Who knows when they're comin' home. Of course, my Daddy could beat the shit out of him, but then Daddy would probably lose his job 'cause Jim's Daddy is a big shot at the company. We can't afford that. If my Daddy lost his job, we'd all starve for sure."

June looked down at the ground and sighed. "Truth is, Lou, I can't say he raped me; I wanted *it* as much as he did. And I couldn't bear to see him hurt, even if he doesn't want me. You can't make somebody love you, so, if he don't want me and my baby, there's nothin' I can do about it".

"You really love him, don't you!"

June hesitated and lowered her head. "Yeah, I guess I do. Sometimes I just want to belong. To have somebody . . . somebody I can count on. Yeah, I do."

Mary Lou nodded sympathetically. "June, if I was you, I'd talk to him as soon as you can. You need to know where you stand."

"I know, Lou, I've put it off too long. I guess I've been afraid to hear what he might say. And then there's Mommy. She'll swear I'm goin' straight to hell!"

She gritted her teeth and fumed, "God, how I hate being stuck like this. Sometimes I wish I was born a man. It must be peachy to go wherever you want . . . do whatever you want . . . have somebody wait on you hand and foot—and never have to worry about getting pregnant!"

"June, I watched my daddy tryin' to make a living and 'fore long I realized life's not fair, period. Sure, most men don't have it easy either, but I watched my momma too and I learned real fast that, for poor folks like us, a woman's life is double not fair. It's hard to find a man who will take care of you and won't knock you around. Let's cross our fingers that Jim'll do you right. Will you come back and see me after you talk to him?"

June brightened up. She smiled at her friend and nodded, "Sure, Lou. I will."

June gazed at the sleeping baby and perked up. "Say, Lou, how's little Ginnie doing?"

"Good. She's a good baby, June. I hope yours is as good as Ginnie."

"Me too. And healthy." June looked hard at her friend. "Lou, what's it like being a mother?"

"It's good, June . . . real good." She took a deep breath, "But it's mighty hard."

As June walked slowly back to Grays Knob lost in thought, she faced a sickning rush of emotions. She was vulnerable, helpless, desperate, anxious and angry all at once. She felt utterly alone. Betrayed. Foolish. One way or the other, she had to talk to Jim Gordon soon.

When June was out of sight, Mary Lou hugged her baby tightly and stroked its soft brown curls. She slumped back in her chair and sobbed as tears began to fall. Like June, her future was clouded with uncertainty.

She didn't have the heart to tell June that Richie had left her almost two months before. She couldn't put it off any longer. She had no choice but to see her parents and plead with them to let her and her baby move in with them.

Pregnant!

When June was finally past her morning sicknesses and was beginning to show, her mother got more short-tempered and critical. June stayed outside and away from the house as much as she could so as not to irritate her mother. It was obvious from the tone of her mother's voice and the dirty looks she gave June that Rhoda was about to explode.

One morning after June had finished cleaning up the breakfast dishes, her mother sat her down in front of the fireplace. "We need to talk," she said, her voice betraying a mixture of anger and worry. "You're pregnant, aren't you?"

Like all the nights after June had realized she was pregnant, she hadn't slept well. *Not now*, she thought. *I can't deal with your hatefulness now.*

"Yes, Mommy, it appears that I am." She drew back and partially covered her eyes, expecting her mother to slap her.

"Dear God, why have you acted so stupidly? Didn't you stop to think what people will say about you and our whole family?" She shook her head in disgust. "Jim Gordon is the father, ain't he?"

"Yes, Mommy, he is."

She scowled at June. "I didn't like that man the first time I laid eyes on him. I knew he was up to no good. Have you talked to him about your baby?"

"No, Mommy, I haven't."

"Well, don't you think it's time you did?"

"Yes, I guess it is." *How long had it been since she had seen him?* As the days dragged by, she had pushed the question out of her mind but now she was forced to confront the truth: she hadn't seen or heard from him in four weeks—and she was feeling uneasy about their relationship. Between bouts of anger and hurt brought on by feeling abandoned and betrayed, she kept hoping she would hear from him.

"Does he even know you're pregnant?" her mother asked. The sarcasm in her voice shattered what was left of June's self esteem.

June spit out the words, "No. I haven't told him yet. Actually, I haven't heard from him in two months."

"Oh, God, I knew it." She shook her head and turned away from her daughter in disgust. "You never listen, do you?"

When she turned to face her daughter again, there were tears stinging her eyes and her face was flushed with anger. "You're bringing shame on this family and God is going to punish you for what you've done. I've prayed for God to deliver us from the shame you're bringing on us. And that you would learn your lesson."

There was a small pile of firewood near the fireplace and June braced herself for the physical assault that was coming.

"Mommy, I'll get Jerry to take me to see Jim. Then I'll decide what to do."

"Well, that baby will be here in four months, whether you're ready or not, so you'd better get something worked out. I'll tell Jerry to take you there tomorrow. He can pick up some flour for me while he's there."

When June and her older brother Jerry arrived at the company store in Alva, he went in to buy the flour and she went to the desk clerk and asked to see Mr. Gordon. "Oh, I remember you. June Brittian, right?"

"Yes, that's right."

The clerk smiled and said, "I'll tell him you're here."

When Jim Gordon finally appeared, he seemed surprised but glad to see her. He led her back to his office and motioned for her to take a seat.

She knew better than to expect any display of affection from him in his office. "I've missed you," she said, lowering her voice.

"I've missed you too," he said. "I'm sorry I've been so busy lately. Our tax returns are due in a few weeks and I've got a lot to do to get them ready."

The thought crossed her mind: *Oh, you're too busy to tell me you really want to see me but you're going to have to disappear for a few weeks because of your job. But we will get together after taxes.*

She bit her tongue, hoping he would say they could get together on the weekend. When he didn't offer to see her, she said, "Jim, I really need to talk to you."

"Yes, of course. I just don't know when I can get away." Her expression turned cold; he could tell she wasn't taking that well.

"I mean right now, God damn it!"

He softened his tone, hoping to calm her down. "Okay. I've got a few minutes now. What do you want to talk about?"

She lowered her voice again. "Jim, I'm pregnant with your baby."

He sat back in his chair and studied her without saying a word or showing any kind of reaction. Finally he said, "You're sure it's mine?"

That was too much for her. Her face flushed. "God damnit, of course, it's yours, you son uva bitch. You know I haven't slept with anyone else," she exploded and jabbed her finger at him. "I told you I didn't believe in having sex before marriage, but you insisted. I told you my mother would kill me if I got pregnant, but you insisted. What kind of man are you!"

He held up his hands, pleading. "June, please keep your voice down."

"Well, we've got a problem because it's your baby and when that baby's born, there won't be any doubt that it's your baby."

Finally he said, "So . . . do you really want to have the baby? I can help you work something out."

"You mean an abortion?"

"Well, yes. After all, we're not married."

"Jim, are you crazy? I'm not gonna' have an abortion. I love you and I'm going to have this baby."

He raised his hands. "All right, suppose I pick you up on Sunday afternoon about 3:00 and we can talk about it."

She calmed down and settled back in her chair. "All right, Jim, I know you'll do the right thing. I'll see you Sunday."

She left his office with tears in her eyes and sat down in the lobby to wait on her brother. She slouched down in her chair and avoided looking at anyone. At first she felt hopeful, then she felt the sting of rejection and betrayal again for the hundredth time.

When Jerry pulled out of the parking lot, he asked her what was wrong. She told him Jim Gordon had insisted on having sex with her. Now she was pregnant and she was afraid he was going to dump her. She told him she was going to see Gordon on Sunday when he was going to tell her what he intended to do.

"Sis," Jerry said, "Do you want me to talk to him? Maybe I can persuade him to do the right thing."

"I don't know," she sighed and closed her eyes. "I just don't know what to do. Let me see what he has to say on Sunday."

That evening Jim Gordon stopped by his parent's house for dinner. After dinner, the young man's demeanor turned serious. He said to his father and mother, "I need to talk to you. I have a problem—you might say an indiscretion on my part."

His father and mother glanced at each other, curiously concerned. Jim Senior gave his son a beer and they sat down together.

Jim Junior cleared his throat and began, "For several months, I've been dating a young woman whose father is one of our miners. Her name is June Brittian. Now she's pregnant and she says the baby is mine. I believe her. I don't think she's been with anyone else. But I don't know how to handle this situation."

Both of his parents were stunned. Finally, his mother said, "My dear Lord, Jim, do you love her?"

Jim looked at his parents solemnly before saying, "I care for her a lot; I mean I do love her. It's just that I'm not sure I want to be married now—and have a baby to take care of."

"Well, son", his father said, "Sounds to me like you've gotten yourself in a fine pickle. What do you intend to do?"

His mother interrupted. "Son, you don't intend to marry that girl, do you? I mean do you even know her that well?"

His father interrupted. "Marlene, the young woman's pregnant and apparently our son is the father. Maybe marrying her is the right thing to do."

He turned to his son. "Tell us about her, Jimmy."

Jim Junior studied the floor, carefully parsing his feelings. "Her mother is a stern old lady, ready to call down the wrath of God on anyone who displeases her. She's one of those Pentecostal snake handlers who doesn't spare the rod. But her father seems to be a good man—doesn't say much. I hear he's a hard worker."

He took a drink and solemnly continued. "As for June, well, she's attractive. She's 18 years old, with a temper. From a poor family that lives in a little log cabin in the hollow at Gray's Knob. June is pretty smart, but she only made it through the fourth grade. I do believe she loves me."

"Well, of course, she loves you," his mother interrupted. "What young woman wouldn't? Sounds to me like she's looking for someone to support her."

Jim senior frowned at his wife. "Marlene, isn't that what women are supposed to do—fall in love with men who will support them? And aren't men supposed to fall in love with women they want to support as their wives? I don't think anyone's to blame here. It's just that they lost control of their passions."

"Jim, you're right but our son here has a bright future ahead of him and he deserves a woman he can be proud of. One who is proper and knows how to be a good wife."

"Marlene, have you forgotten how *hot* we were when we were Jimmy's age! We were crazy about each other, and you didn't care what it meant to be proper. We were lucky that . . ."

Her face flushed. "All right, Jim, you've made your point, but we were careful! The real issue here is whether or not our son loves her—enough to marry her and be a father to her child." She turned to her son, "Do you, Jimmy?"

Jim Junior rubbed his forehead methodically and considered the question. "I do care for her a lot but I'm just not ready to take on a family."

His mother pursed her lips tightly and almost whispered, "Well then, what about an abortion?"

"It's out of the question. She won't even consider it."

"All right, what about letting someone adopt it?" his mother asked.

"I don't think she'll go for that either," he sighed. "She's stubborn."

All three of them mulled over the situation without comment.

Finally, Jim Senior said, "I can't insist that you marry her if you don't love her but I also can't bear the thought of your child going hungry or growing up destitute. I think the honorable thing to do is to be honest about the situation and offer to support her. After all, you do bear some responsibility in this situation."

He turned to his wife. "Well, Marlene, what do you think?"

She regarded her son with a comforting look. "I suppose that makes sense. But, Jimmy, can you even afford to help her financially? I mean should you take on that responsibility since—I'm quite sure—she led you on?"

Jim Junior considered her question and chose his words carefully. "I wouldn't say that June led me on . . . I mean It just happened." He paused and studied the floor. "I will admit I felt bad about it afterwards. He looked up at his father and grimaced. "I guess I was quite insistent in the heat of the moment."

The conversation went back and forth without reaching a decision about the best thing to do so they decided to talk about it again on another day.

It was a bitterly cold Sunday afternoon on a damp and dreary day in January with a hint of snow when Jimmy Gordon arrived at the Brittian cabin. He wore a pair of jeans and a heavy woolen coat that afforded ample protection from the chill. When he knocked on the door, June answered and invited him in and gave him a lingering hug. Then she led him to the stone fireplace where her mother huddled by a dying fire, reading her heavy and worn old King James bible, the one source of comfort in her troubled life.

He noticed June's coat was pitifully threadbare, too thin to offer much protection from the cold. When he spoke to June's mother, she only acknowledged him by nodding stoically and continued reading.

He felt a twinge of shame. "Let's go to Fred's and get something to eat," he whispered to June.

She nodded her head *Yes* and turned to her mother. "Can we bring you something from town?"

Her mother shook her head *No* without looking up.

When June and Jim walked into Fred's Diner on the outskirts of Harlan, it was almost empty. They seated themselves at a corner table that allowed them some privacy and ordered two mugs of steaming hot chocolate while they looked over the menu. They sat in awkward silence for a couple of minutes, each one hesitant to speak first.

Jim cleared his throat. "Your mom knows you're pregnant, doesn't she?"

June sighed, "Sure she does. She's not stupid."

"She's given you hell about it, hasn't she?"

"Yeah. Apparently, I've committed a mortal sin that will send me straight to hell."

That statement struck him as unjustified and plain ridiculous. He knew June loved him—she had told him as much and showed it. *If she was going to hell because, in her youthful innocence, she had loved him too much, what,* he wondered, *would happen to him?*

The answer came to him quickly: *Nothing. Nothing will happen to me. That's the way it's meant to be.* He felt sorry about it but that was fate, wasn't it? *There's nothing I can do about that.* He looked back at June, stung by the realization that he was leaving her to deal with the consequences of their unrestrained passion. It bothered him.

He tried to make light of the situation: "Well, if you're going to hell, then I guess there's no hope for me: I expect I'll go to the hottest part."

She was not amused.

He pushed on clumsily: "Look, I do love you but I'm just not ready to take on a family now."

"I wish you had told me that before we had sex."

"I'm sorry, June. I didn't mean to lead you on."

She was looking at him intently, waiting, her eyes pleading for some measure of reassurance. Finally she put her hand on his and said, almost in a whisper, "Jim, it's your baby too. What are you going to do?"

He avoided her eyes, seeming lost in thought. "June, I honestly don't know."

She was crushed. She felt abandoned, like she had fallen down a well and no one was there to save her. Grasping at one last straw, she said, "I guess you've talked to your parents. What do they say?"

"If you don't want to have an abortion, my father suggests that I give you some financial support. I'm agreeable with that. Given some time I'm sure I could grow to love you and the baby."

She looked at him aghast and shaken to the core. "Given some time!" she snapped, trying hard to bite her tongue and conceal her hurt.

He leaned in close to her and lowered his voice. "If you want to have an abortion, of course, I'll pay for it."

The waitress came to take their orders but they had no appetite. He sat up straight and waved her away.

"Jim, I'm not having an abortion." She leaned in close to him and spit out the words: "I don't want . . . I will NOT have an abortion! I'm not giving up OUR baby." For an instant she teetered on the verge of calling him every vile name she could think of, but her anger quickly gave way to despair.

He threw up his hands. "All right. You're going to need money for yourself and for the baby. Suppose I give you $200.00 to cover the cost of the delivery, baby clothes, some clothes for yourself and medicine. No, no, you'll need more than that. Suppose I give you $400.00. What do you think of that?"

"Well, that's mighty kind but, more than money, that baby's gonna' need a father."

"June, I can't be that baby's father . . . Uhh, there's something I need to tell you."

Oh, God, she thought, expecting the worst. *Is he in love with someone else?* "What?" she said, bracing herself.

He took a deep breath. "I'm going to be moving back to Tennessee. In a couple of weeks. To take another job. One that pays better . . . of, course, I'll stay in touch."

There it was. She would have their baby by herself. She felt sick to her stomach. There wasn't anything left to say so he took her home.

When she walked in the door, it wasn't late. Her mother was still sitting by the fireplace. She looked up at her daughter, for the first time sensing the depth of her pain. "He's not gonna' marry you, is he?"

"No, Mommy, he's not."

A Baby

T hursday January 21, 1944. Lily Darby had just sat down with her family to a dinner of pinto beans, fried tomatoes and corn bread when someone knocked on their front door. "I'll get it," Lily said as she pushed back from the table and stood up.

Her father nodded and wrinkled his nose. "It's probably Preacher Purl checking on us since we missed church on Sunday."

When she opened the door, June Brittian was standing there, looking panicked, with tears running down her cheeks. "Lil', I've got to talk to you," she blurted out.

"June, what's wrong?" Lily said, worried.

June lifted the hem of her skirt to show the red welts on the backs of her legs.

Lily covered her mouth with her hand in shock. "June, we just sat down to dinner. Please come in and join us."

June shook her head no. "I'm a mess. I don't want your mom and dad to see me like this."

"All right. Wait over there by the swing and I'll hurry."

June hugged her tightly. "Thanks, Lily, I don't know what I'd do if I didn't have you as my friend," she said as she turned towards the swing.

Lily closed the door and went back to the table. "It's June. She's got a bad beatin'. She wants me to go for a walk with her."

"What did June get a whippin for, Lil'?", Joshua asked, looking worried.

Lily's mother put her forefinger to her lips and hissed at him. "Josh', Shush!"

"Rhoda is just too hard on her girls," Lily's father said with a frown.

"Well, tell her to come in and have supper with us," her mother said.

"I did, Momma, but she's too ashamed to come in." Lily studied her mother for a minute. "She looks awfully hungry, Momma. Can I take her something to eat?"

Her father spoke up. "'Course, you can, Lil'. Take her some beans and corn bread." He shook his head. "That little gal is skinnier than a fence post."

Lily filled two bowls with pinto beans, added two pieces of corn bread, two onions, some canned tomatoes and a couple of spoons and headed for the door. "I'll be back before dark," she said.

Her little brother interrupted. "Can I come too?"

Lily stooped down in front of him and smiled. "No, Josh, not this time. We've got some girl talkin' to do."

Lily handed June a bowl of beans. "Here. We'll have supper together."

June took the food and thanked Lily. She picked at her food.

"You got another beatin'! What for this time? Did you sass your Momma again?"

June held her bowl in one hand and rubbed her tummy with the other. "This is why," she sobbed.

"You're pregnant!" Lily gasped. "Does Jim know?"

Her face dropped. "Yeah, he knows."

"So . . ."

"He don't want to talk about it. Everything changed when I told him I was pregnant."

"Don't tell me that sorry son of a bitch is leavin' you high and dry! 'June Bug', what're you going to do?"

"Lil', I don't know. I swear I must be the stupidest girl in the world: I thought he loved me."

"What does your Momma say?"

"She don't say nothin', 'cause she ain't talkin' to me. She mostly just ignores me, looks mad and wanders around mutterin' to herself. She must be talkin' to the Lord about the situation, but I don't think He's talkin' to her, and He sure ain't talkin' to me."

"What about your dad?"

"He called Jim a son of a bitch. Then he said he would figure something out. But there's nothing he can do. He can't stir up a fuss and risk losing his job. Besides, it's too embarrassing. Everybody at the mine would hear about it and call me a tramp. The thing is I can't stay at home any more. Before I get much bigger, I'll have to leave."

"Your mom's kickin' you out!"

"Yeah, she says I've disgraced the family. I'm afraid she's goin' to run me off ."

"Will your Daddy let her do that?"

"I don't know . . . maybe. He can't do a whole lot with her. But it don't matter . . . I can't go and I can't stay. She'll make my life miserable either way."

"Where will you go?"

"I don't know. She might send me to Aunt Mary's but I'd as soon go to hell as go there. I'm terrified to have that baby in some strange place. At least if I had it here, you'd be close by." She paused to collect her thoughts. "Lil', . . ."

"What?"

"You won't tell your folks I'm pregnant, will you?"

"If you don't want me to, I won't."

"Thanks, Lil'. I don't know what I would do if you weren't my friend."

"Well, are you goin' to keep that baby?"

"Of course, I'm goin' to keep it. That's my baby and I ain't givin' it up for nobody."

"Well, how are you goin' to keep it? You don't have a husband or a job."

"I don't know but I'll find a way."

Lily studied on the situation for a minute. "June, what will I tell my folks if they ask about you?"

"I don't know, Lil'. I don't know but I'll think of somethin'."

When June walked in, it was almost dark. Her father had dozed off in their small bedroom in their decrepit old rocker and her mother was waiting for her, clearly livid. "Where have you been?" she demanded.

"Talking to Lily," June replied defiantly.

"Did you tell her you were pregnant?"

"No," she lied.

Her mother rolled her eyes with contempt. "Well, you'd better not tell anybody if you know what's good for you. Now, here's what we're gonna' do. You're goin' to have to leave soon. I'll see if Aunt Mary will take you in for a few months—until after you've had the baby. She'll find a granny midwife for you in Lee County. I expect somebody will be glad to adopt it."

"Nooo! I ain't givin' up my baby," June wailed. "I don't want to have my baby at Aunt Mary's. Don't you have any feelin's for me at all!"

Her mother grabbed her by the hair of her head and leaned over her, raising her voice. "June, you listen to me. What on God's Earth is Preacher Purl goin' to think of us? You can't raise that baby by yourself."

Her father appeared in the doorway, aroused by the commotion, looking upset. He had almost fallen out of the rocking chair. He was unshaven and his hair was a mess. "Rhodie, don't be so hard on her. I don't give a damn what people think about us. And I'll be damned if you're going to send her off to Mary's to have her baby. She needs to be here where we can look after her."

"And have everybody talkin' about us behind our backs because our daughter had a baby out of wedlock!" She curled her lip and raised her voice: "I won't have it."

"Rhodie, I mean it: you can't send her away. We'll get her a midwife right here in Harlan County. Granny Lou will do it."

"Well, John, how do you think we're going to feed another mouth? If there's another strike, we're all goin' to starve! And how are we goin' to pay to have the baby delivered."

June turned to her father, pleading. "Daddy, I'll leave as soon as my baby's born. I'll go to Louisville and get a job. You won't have my mouth to feed and I'll take my baby with me as soon as it's old enough. I'll pay Granny Lou somehow." She was hoping Jim would pay the expenses for delivering her baby but she knew she couldn't count on it.

Her father put his arms around his daughter and kissed her on the forehead. She felt so small and vulnerable and he knew she was hurting. "June, Honey, don't worry. We'll make sure you keep your baby and we'll be as proud of it as we can be."

He looked at his wife sternly and arched his eyebrows. "Won't we, Rhodie?"

In a huff, Rhoda turned around, stomped into the bedroom and slammed the door.

For the next three months there was an uneasy and volatile truce between June, supported by her father, and her mother. Some days her mother spent the day in tears; other days she was sullen and berated June. And some days she totally ignored June as if she didn't exist. That was the most painful of all for June because she felt like a failure and worthless.

Late one Saturday afternoon in March, two weeks before she was due, her mother, frustrated and angry, pulled her aside. "We've got to talk to your father and do something. Like it or not, that baby's coming in two weeks or sooner and you better get ready for it. I wrote Aunt Mary and asked if you could stay with them a spell. She said she would be glad to have you stay with them for as long as need be. They have a big house and plenty of room. Your father can drive you over there on a Sunday. It's no more than a four hour drive."

June was stunned. "I don't want to go over there and have my baby with a bunch of strangers gawkin' at my every move." She ran to her room and began to sob, "I don't want to go."

Her mother looked toward heaven, rolled her eyes and shook her head. "Sweet Jesus, what am I going to do with her?"

When John Brittian came home, he could feel the tension in the air. "What's wrong, Rhodie?" he asked, dreading to hear why she was upset.

"John, it's less than two weeks before June is due. She's refusin' to go to Mary's. We've got to decide what to do. She insists on having the baby here."

His face and hands were black with coal dust and sweat. "Well, why can't she?" he snapped. He slumped down in the creaky old rocking chair, leaned back and closed his eyes. "Why can't she, Rhodie? I reckon she's all grown up, ain't she?"

She was out of patience and once more in a huff. "John, you know why she can't stay here."

He looked up at her, exasperated. "Hell fire, Rhodie, we ain't gonna' turn our daughter away no matter what people say. Find Granny Lou and get her to come here when the baby's due."

He lapsed into silence, so tired he could hardly move or find the will to speak. With calloused fingers he rubbed his temples and stared transfixed into the dying red flames that danced back and forth in the small fireplace.

Rhoda grew impatient. "John, we can't . . ."

John interrupted her. "Rhodie, you heard me—we ain't sendin' our daughter away. What do you think Christ would have us do?"

Oh, how that man frustrated her. She put her hands on her hips and spit the words at him, "Well, I do declare; behold the man who never darkens a church house door! So you're the one to tell me what Christ would say!" Furious, she bit her tongue and left the room.

Granny Lou, otherwise known as Louisa Josephine Graham to those few who knew her full name, was one of a handful of midwives in Harlan County. She was a skinny little colored woman in her sixties who was wise and tougher than she looked; she had learned the skills of midwifery from the time she was eight years old at her mothers side.

If the mother was unwed, Granny Lou also served as her confessor and confidante. She had heard so many woeful tales of men abandoning their women after getting them pregnant, as her man had done, that her opinion of men in general was as low as a frog's belly.

A lot of folks in Harlan County lived so far back in hollows or remote areas accessible by such poor roads that reaching a hospital was a long and wearisome ordeal. On the other hand, a midwife could deliver a baby right there in the mother's home where she's more comfortable, undisturbed by all the strangers and the commotion going on around her in a hospital.

Besides that, a doctor might charge $50.00 for a delivery, an awful lot of money to a coal miner's family, while Granny Lou charged $2.50. If a family was really poor, she didn't mind accepting a couple of chickens or a bushel of corn or potatoes as payment.

Granny Lou considered childbirth a natural process that worked best when Nature was allowed to take its course without undue interference. She was convinced that, when it came to having babies, women usually fared better without doctors or hospitals. She recommended ginger tea for morning sickness. For the actual delivery, her tools were simple and few: a notebook to record the births, a sharp butcher knife, a pair of scissors, a bar of soap, hot water and a few clean rags.

The only problem with using a midwife was that most of them didn't use anesthetics such as ether and chloroform. Granny Lou, like most midwives, believed it was women's fate to suffer due to the "curse of Eve"; thus pain during childbirth was to be expected because it was God's will. For some unknown reason that meant that poor women suffered the pain of childbirth far more than the well off.

On April 1, 1944, with Granny Lou's skilled assistance, June gave birth to a healthy son at home. She named him Samuel after her beloved brother and called him "Sammy".

JUNE'S FIRST BORN — AS A CHILD AND AS AN ADULT

Sammy — Born 1944

Sam Bledsoe, Midshipman
NROTC Univ. N. Carolina

A Bad Marriage

By February of 1945, Sammy was almost a year old and June was desperate. Her welcome with her mother was wearing thin so June made up her mind she had to find either a husband or a job soon. She dreaded the thought of leaving her baby but it was obvious her mother had not forgiven her and the tension between them was hard for her to endure. Besides that, she saw how unhappy her friend Mary Lou was living with her parents. That would not do for her she firmly decided.

The one bright spot in her situation was that her parents had bonded with their new grandson so Rhoda readily agreed to take care of him while she looked for a job. They gave her what little money they could spare. It was just enough for a one-way bus ticket to Louisville and food for about a week.

June decided Louisville would be the best place to look for a job while her parents took care of Sammy. And the Fort Knox Army base was nearby with several thousand young and lonely soldiers.

Shortly after arriving in Louisville, she found a job that barely paid the rent for a small appartment and enough food for a couple of meals a day. She learned where some of the servicemen hung out and met a young soldier named Al Bowers at a popular tavern in the city.

Bowers was a fairly good-looking guy and a smooth talker from Pennsylvania. He took a liking to her and asked her for a date. She soon noticed a few traits that bothered her: he seemed to enjoy his booze too much, he was flirty, he was careless with his money and he tended to be pushy, even controlling. But she was desperate and he seemed to genuinely care for her.

Three months later they were married. After a hectic weekend honeymoon, June was missing Sammy and eager to realize her dream of being part of a happy family. Eventually Bowers gave in and reluctantly agreed that she could bring little Sammy to live with them.

But after they brought Sammy to Louisville, Bowers was not thrilled when it registered that June's baby required a lot of her attention. It became apparent that he was not ready to be a father; a baby was an inconvenience, a complication and an expense he didn't wish to contend with.

For her part, June realized her new husband was more interested in spending money on booze than on his family. To make matters worse, his abusive nature soon revealed itself. He was an enlisted man in the Army who wasn't making much money, so he made up his mind that supporting a wife—AND a baby—was a greater responsibility than he cared to take on. Because she had a baby to care for, she wasn't able to get a job; his insistence that she go to work created more tension and sparked heated arguments between them.

Finally after six contentious months, Al Bowers decided after one of his drinking bouts that he definitely did not want to be a father any longer. June was waiting when he came home drunk near midnight to their apartment and she was furious. They had a bitter argument; he told her, "Either the baby goes or I go."

But she wasn't going to give up her baby for anybody. "Then you're the one going, you son of a bitch!" she screamed. He slept on the couch and the next morning he was gone. That was the last time she saw Al Bowers.

Rejected and on her own again, she was distraught. Overwhelmed and hopeless, she threw herself on the bed and cried for a long time. She thought about her experiences with men—they were all bad. *You can't depend on a man*, she thought. *You can't trust them to take any responsibility. They will use you for sex and then leave you.*

Since June's job prospects were not good and she was running out of money, she was forced to return to Harlan. She would have to persuade her parents to take in her baby son again until she could find some way to support him.

Women had few job opportunities except in teaching or secretarial work and she had no qualifications in those fields. She could expect no more than eventually finding a menial job paying very little or moving back in with her parents. She would have to try again to find a husband.

She thought of her little sister Ruth, barely 13 years old. *Maybe Ruth can look after Sammy until I can get on my feet. What would I do without her?* She thought. Ruth was responsible and mature for a 13-year old, far more so than any boys she had ever seen.

After the end of her brief marriage to Al Bowers, June returned home to spend time with Sammy and figure out what to do next. As soon as she managed to scrape together enough money, she would have to leave again to find either a decent job or a decent husband. In the meantime, Sammy and Ruth had bonded. June turned to her little sister once again.

The war in Europe was over. Germany had surrendered on May 7 and the war against Japan was drawing to a close in the Pacific. Sixteen million Americans, almost all men, had served in the war, and they would be coming home soon. That was great news for all of the women back home and for the men, but all of those men would need jobs.

One Wednesday Rosalie Bean, a lady from church, stopped by to spend the morning with June's mother in Bible study. Rosalie brought her daughter Ellie, who was a year younger than June, with her so the girls could visit. June discovered that Ellie lived in Verne with her parents and that she was also discouraged about living at home and as desperate as June to find a husband.

After managing to get together a few more times, they became fast friends. With World War II over, they knew millions of service men would be passing through the major train stations all over the country on their way home so the two of them excitedly hatched a plan.

June and Ellie scraped together what little money they could to buy two one-way tickets to Cincinnati and strike out on their own. But Ellie's mother discovered their plan and, fearful for her daughter's safety, forbade her daughter to leave. Her father refused to even let her talk to June.

This was a setback June had not anticipated. Once more she was faced with a dilemma: what could she do?

Kenneth, Raymond, Mary and Walter

The Bledsoe Clan

M uch about Walter Murray Bledsoe is a mystery. He was born on July 17, 1897 in Rockwood, a small town some 25 miles west of Knoxville in east Tennessee.

Walter was a smallish but wiry man who was stern and easily riled. He was never heard to express a compliment, show affection, or crack a joke. He had an older brother Richard who lived in Rockwood and a younger sister Jean who lived in Lima, Ohio. His father was William E. Bledsoe; his mother was Mary Ann Francis. Apparently none of them were close to Walter for they rarely, if ever, visited him as far as his neighbors knew.

Except for that meager information, nothing more is known about his parents or his siblings. Indeed Walter was never heard to speak a single word about them. Actually this is not a totally accurate statement for one anecdote is known about Walter's brother Richard.

In 1966, Richard and a friend were struck and killed under mysterious circumstances by a Southern Railway train passing through Rockwood as they dallied along the tracks at 11:00 in the morning. They failed to respond to the sounds of the approaching train until it was too late. The bodies were a bloody mangled mess. Richard was 74 and his friend was 67 at the time of their deaths and both men left families behind. How such a bizarre and senseless tragedy could happen was uncertain but there were rumors that the two were drunk while arguing or playing chicken.

Walter and Richard were not close and rarely talked even though they lived only a few miles apart. So, in one sense, it was not surprising that Walter showed little emotion about the loss of his brother.

In 1923, Walter met, under unknown circumstances, and married 21-year old Mary Almeda Fuller—a kindhearted and gentle woman, thoroughly steeped in religion—also from Rockwood, in 1929. She came from a fairly well-off and educated family. Three of her six siblings were secondary school teachers. Her father Johnce Caldwell Fuller owned substantial acreage in the small community of Post Oak Springs and was highly respected in the area.

It would be hard to find a husband and wife with less in common. Mary was as calm and friendly as he was volatile and unsocial. She was as trusting as he was suspicious. No wonder most people from her church and her family considered their marriage to be a poor match. Walter made little effort to interact with his wife's family even though they lived close by in Post Oak Springs.

Most people agreed that Walter was hard to get to know. He was socially awkward and tended to regale those he met with stories about doing some mundane task better than anyone else while he made little effort to get to know his listener. He was never heard to pay a compliment to his long suffering wife. Once when Mary tried on a new shade of red lipstick, Walter declared that her mouth reminded him of the ass end of a blue jay that had eaten poke berries. He had not completed high school and was not a proficient reader; that fact may have fed feelings of inferiority and contributed to his suspicious nature.

The Fullers were strong supporters of the small Post Oak Springs Christian Church which Mary attended regularly her entire life. Her faith was simple and unquestioning while unwavering; Walter, on the other hand, never went to church with her, showing no interest in matters of religion. Their marriage suffered a long, rocky period after Walter accused her and the preacher, and later a deacon, of having an affair.

He was also given to bouts of drinking which brought out the meanness in him. When he was "mean drunk", sometimes he would terrify Mary by shooting up the house with his shotgun. She would have to run and hide in a nearby ditch until he sobered up.

In 1934, Walter bought from Mary's father, J. C. Fuller, the land on which he would build their house in 1937 with the address 269 Old Kingston Highway in Post Oak Springs community. Walter and Mary lived in that modest two-bedroom frame house from the day they moved in until the day they died, except for a brief time at the end of her life when she went into a nursing home. There, directly across the highway from the Winter Haven Tourist Camp, they raised two rather handsome sons: Kenneth Walter, born in 1924, and Raymond Stanley, born in 1927.

In spite of their father's stern influence, both boys were good hearted with generous nature. But Kenneth was more level-headed and responsible while Raymond tended toward exaggeration and enjoyed being the center of attention. He also displayed some of the social awkwardness of his father.

Walter was a hard worker who demanded no less from his wife and two sons. He worked as a mechanic at the hosiery mill in Harriman and raised most of the family's food on their small farm by keeping a garden and raising chickens. He was an excellent fisherman but he never took his sons or his grandsons fishing.

Mary kept house and canned vegetables from their garden. The boys helped with the gardening and drew their water from a spring in the nearby hollow. There were always chores to be done and, when the boys failed to meet his expectations, he didn't hesitate to use his blacksnake whip on them. He had a mule named "Dolly" that he used to plow his garden and he beat his boys mercilessly, just like he did Dolly, when he believed they were too slack in doing their chores.

World War II was raging across Europe in 1943, when Kenneth was 19. One day when his father was using Dolly to plow his garden plot, Kenneth couldn't bear the cruel way his father continued beating Dolly, even after she collapsed. The ground was hard and Dolly was old so Kenneth pleaded with his father to stop; instead his father started beating him. But Kenneth had become an adult and it was the last straw. He grabbed his father by the wrists and swore, "That's the last damn time you're ever going to beat me!"

It was the last time his father ever saw his older son alive. The next day Kenneth joined the Army. Kenneth was inducted into the Army just across the state line in Fort Oglethorpe, Georgia. He received orders to report to Camp Wheeler, Georgia for training and upon completion of his training was assigned to the 29th Infantry Division in Europe.

His father was so furious that Kenneth had stood up to him that he essentially disowned Kenneth and refused to correspond with him. Kenneth wrote to his mother as often as he could but not to his father. Father and son would never again have contact with one another.

His mother was broken hearted that her husband and son were estranged, that her husband in effect had disowned their son and refused to correspond with him.

In September of 1944, Mary received the following letter from Tennessee's Congressman in Washington:

Dear Mrs. Bledsoe:

I am advised by the War Department that your son, Pfc Kenneth W. Bledsoe, is reported missing in action. I wish to express to you my deepest sympathy and the hope that you may later learn that your son is safe.

I want you to feel free to call upon me to render any assistance within my power here in Washington.

Sincerely yours,

Representative John Jennings, Jr.

That news brought her many sleepless nights. It prompted a torrent of tears and a string of prayers. But Mary's prayers were not answered. In October of 1944, she received a posthumous citation from 29th Infantry Headquarters awarding her son the Bronze Star medal:

PFC Kenneth W. Bledsoe, 116th Infantry, U S Army, for meritorious achievement in military operations against the enemy in Normandy, France. On 8 June 1944 Pfc Bledsoe, Automatic Rifleman, excelled in the performance of duty during the early stages of the Normandy beachhead. Displaying courage and aggressiveness, he provided effective covering fire for the advancing troops until killed by enemy machine gun fire. Pfc Bledsoe's unselfish devotion to duty reflects great credit upon himself and the Military Service.

Her sorrow was almost more than she could bear. "Dead and only 20 years old! Dear God, How can it be?" she cried, desperate to understand.

The following weeks were difficult for Mary as she grieved over the loss of her son. They were also painful for Raymond because he idolized his older brother. Walter on the other hand simply declared that runnin' off to join the Army was a foolish thing to do and never talked about the death of his first-born.

In November, the telegram came: their son was coming home. Kenneth was coming home . . . in a casket. To be laid to rest and mourned by his small family. He never had the chance to have a wife and children to love him. His nephews and niece would be born too late to ever know him. And as the years went by, his family would rarely ever mention him—remembering was too painful.

He was a devoted son, a protective brother and a good man who made the ultimate sacrifice for his country and too soon would be forgotten. But Kenneth was coming home.

Over the years, Walter's drinking bouts worsened and he became more belligerent and unpredictable. Sometimes when he was drunk, she would have to run for her life and hide in a nearby ditch until he sobered up. In spite of his continuing abusiveness and alcoholism, she never considered divorcing him and never complained. In her mind, God had decreed that the husband was head of the household and was to be obeyed. In spite of her difficult marriage, divorce was not an option.

In 1976, Walter died when he lost control of his pick-up truck, causing it to plunge down a 30-foot embankment and flip over on its top in a creek. A subsequent investigation determined he lost control because one of the wheels locked up.

After Walter's death, Mary lived on by herself for a few more years in the little house as her health declined. Eventually she developed dementia and had to go into a nursing home where she died in 1992.

Mary Almeda Fuller
Born May 9, 1902
Married Sept. 5, 1929
Died July 25, 1992

Walter Murray Bledsoe
Born July 12,1897
Died Feb. 11, 1974

Pfc. Kenneth W. Bledsoe
Born May 28, 1924
KIA June 8,1944

Raymond S. Bledsoe
Born July 23, 1927
Died Oct. 14, 2014

Raymond

June was rattled by the loss of her partner Ellie Bean, but she would not be deterred. She decided to see their plan through although it would mean going it alone. She was still smarting from the dead end relationship with James Gordon and down in the dumps after her failed marriage to Bowers. *Three strikes and you're out*, she thought. *One more chance to hit a home run.* She had to go to Cincinnati—it was her last chance.

She boarded a bus in Harlan and reached Cincinnati the next day on February 17, exhausted after a grueling day and a half long trip. Since she had only a few dollars for food, unless she found a job or a boyfriend soon to help her, she would be in dire financial straits.

June slept in the bus station that night and early on the 18th she carried her bag into the women's restroom and put on the best outfit she could cobble together. It was her 21st birthday but there was nothing to celebrate. She skipped breakfast and set out for Union Terminal. She darted across Western Avenue, and made the long walk down Ezzard Charles Drive past Lincoln Park until she stood before the grandest edifice she had ever seen.

She gazed up in awe at the concrete behemoth that was one of the largest and most impressive train stations in America. Inside she took in a vast openness that was designed to accommodate 17,000 passengers and 216 trains a day, running on schedules around the clock. At its peak in 1944, there were 34,000 soldiers traveling through the terminal each day.

But Union Terminal was far more than a train station; she found a vast waiting area with hundreds of seats and a small city with clothing stores, restaurants, and many other kinds of shops. Coming from the small backwater town of Harlan, Union Terminal with its grand Art Deco style design and magnificent mosaic murals boggled her mind.

She strolled through the huge waiting area, unable to believe her eyes but encouraged. There was indeed a vast crowd of eager servicemen milling around, impatiently passing time between their connections, or browsing through the shops. She had never seen so many young men in one place. She could feel their excitement. The war was over; they were going home. She envied them: they were looking forward to coming home but she was running away from hers.

What am I goin' to do now? she wondered, unable to think straight. She scanned the seats around her and focused on the wide entrance from the platforms. She sat down and tried to collect her thoughts. She reviewed the details of the plan she and Ellie had cooked up.

At last, h er jumbled thoughts coalesced into specific actions: *The passengers come in from the trains over there and walk along this broad aisle past this long row of seats. I'll sit in this section with an empty seat beside me. If a fellow who looks promising comes along and asks if the seat beside me is taken, I'll say no. Then we can strike up a conversation. If I'm clever enough, maybe he'll ask me to go to lunch or dinner with him.*

If a fellow who looks shabby comes along and wants to take the seat beside me, I'll say it's taken, that I'm waitin' on my boyfriend. Why won't that work?

Then it occurred to her: *What if they ask me where I'm going? Hmm,* she thought, *I'll say I've just arrived in Cincinnati and I'm looking for a job.*

She took a seat near the entrance and tried to relax while looking friendly but respectable. At a glance, she could size up any man who approached and showed an interest in her empty seat. If he wore a wedding ring or if he was too fat, shabby, old, loud, pushy or dull, she immediately thought, *No, not him.*

By 4:00 that afternoon, almost 40 men had approached her, but she had given no more than five or six of them the chance to sit next to her and start a conversation. A young Army officer named Paul approached her and asked if the seat beside her was taken. June liked the way he looked and told him it wasn't taken. They chatted and hit it off, but the young man was returning to his home in Raleigh, North Carolina. He glanced at his watch and exclaimed, "Oh, I've got a train to catch. It's been nice talking to you, June. Good luck." Then he rushed away.

At 1:00 in the morning, exhausted and discouraged, June sat upright by herself and tried to keep from nodding off. Several young men approached and chatted briefly but they soon rushed away again to continue their journey back to their families.

In the wee hours of the morning, the terminal was quiet and less crowded. She was tired and so sleepy she couldn't keep from dozing off from time to time. Her whole body was stiff. She stood up, stretched and looked around. Her stomach was growling and she was feeling totally helpless.

She thought, *Life is just one big waiting room where you sit and wait until some guy who can fix your problems comes along and notices you. To hell with love—I need a man who can fix my problems.* She sunk back down in her seat and waited and waited. Every now and then a couple holding hands would stroll by. How she envied them; she had never felt so alone or so unsure of herself.

Eventually a handsome young sailor with brown hair and a big smile sauntered into the terminal and noticed her. "Is this seat taken?" he asked.

She perked up. "No, Sweetheart, it's not," she smiled. "Have a seat."

He was carrying a heavy duffel bag. He set it down in front of his seat, then sat down and breathed a sigh of relief. "Aw, that's better. That bag wears me out. I've hauled it all the way from L.A."

"Looks like you're just out of the Navy. Where are you headed, sailor?" she inquired sweetly.

"Back home to Tennessee," he replied.

She noted he had a fetching smile and dark wavy hair. "Is that so? Where in Tennessee?"

"Rockwood, a little ol' town right outside of Knoxville in the east end of the state. Bet you've never heard of it. Say, where are you headed?"

"Well, I don't know Rockwood but I do know a little about Knoxville. It's not far from my home town of Harlan in Eastern Kentucky. I've been up here in Cincinnati lookin' for a job. Haven't had any luck so I'm trying to decide what to do."

His heart was thumping; she was without a doubt the prettiest woman he had ever laid eyes on. He stuck out his hand. "My name's Raymond Bledsoe—my friends call me 'Ray'. What's your name?"

She shook his hand. "June Brittian. Well, Ray, I guess you've got a lot of family back there in Rockwood."

"Oh, just my parents and some aunts and uncles. And a few cousins. I don't have any brothers or sisters. My brother got killed in France at Normandy. About a year ago."

"Oh, I'm sorry to hear about your brother," she replied, lowering her voice respectfully. "What was his name?"

Raymond hung his head a bit and assumed a more sober tone. "Kenneth," he replied. "I sure do miss him—he was a good brother."

After a brief silence between them, he regarded her hopefully and perked up. "Say, are you hungry? Want to get somethin' to eat?"

"Well, I guess so," she grinned. "Are you buyin'?"

"Sure. Let's go." He remembered his duffel bag. "Oh, I'll have to carry that thing with me," he grinned a little sheepishly.

By the time they had finished eating, they were holding hands. After a couple more hours of talking about all the things they discovered they had in common, they managed a tentative kiss. She confided to him that she had been married before and had a two year old baby son—that didn't faze Raymond—but she neglected to mention that she was not married when she had her baby or that she was not yet divorced from Bowers.

An hour later, they confessed their love for each other and vowed that they couldn't bear to say goodbye to each other. Raymond determined he couldn't risk losing her, even if it meant taking on the responsibility of a wife and a baby. "Look, why don't you come home with me and meet my parents? The train to Knoxville leaves in the morning. I'll buy you a ticket."

"You're crazy!" she laughed. "I can't just run off with somebody I'm not married to—even if I do love him."

He blurted it out: "Well, then let's get married!"

"Are you serious?"

"Well, not today—how about tomorrow? In Knoxville. We love each other, don't we? The train leaves at 8:10. We can sleep on the train!"

They were like two children in a candy store. Raymond bought a one-way ticket for June and imagined how thrilled his parents would be when he and June arrived and he announced that he had gotten married and acquired a baby in the deal. It didn't occur to either of them that his parents might be shocked because he had impetuously married a woman he had just met.

June and Raymond left Cincinnati on the train to Knoxville the next morning. The ride was so noisy and uncomfortable that their sleep was too fitful to be salutary. The next morning they were in Knoxville, tired but excited; they immediately sought out a justice of the peace and got married on February 19, 1946. June had just turned 21 and Raymond was not yet 19.

It was a far bigger gamble than either of them realized. After all, how well can you get to know someone in a matter of hours before you marry them. Nevertheless, they plunged forward with unfounded optimism into their new lives, blissfully unaware of the trials they would confront.

After lunch at a small diner on Magnolia Avenue, they caught a Greyhound bus for the 45 mile trip to Rockwood, arriving late in the afternoon at the Peggy Ann Truck Stop.

Raymond's parents lived only three miles out of town in the Post Oak Community. The couple hitched a ride with a local farmer in a beat up old pickup and 15 minutes later they were standing on the porch of the little house where Raymond grew up. Their clothes were rumpled and their hair was disheveled. The dark rings around their eyes and their grimy, unkempt appearance made it appear they hadn't slept well for days.

When Mary opened the door, she was dumbstruck. She stood there with her mouth open, unable to speak. There was her son with some unknown woman. He gave her a long hug, then motioned for June to step forward. "This is my new wife June, Mama—We met up in Cincinnati." He grinned broadly. "And, uhh, well, we just got married in Knoxville!"

Mary almost fainted but she managed to gather her wits about her. "Hello . . . June?"

"Yes, I'm June, Mrs. Bledsoe. Pleased to meet you. I'm from Harlan, Kentucky."

Mary motioned them inside. There was a table set with two plates for dinner. She hugged Raymond again. "Welcome home, Son," she whispered. "Thank God you're home safely."

Raymond glanced at his watch. "Say, Mama, I guess Pap will be gettin' home from work soon, won't he?"

"Oh, yes, your father still gets home about 5:30."

"Can't wait to see him. Say, we're awfully hungry. Can you put out two more plates for dinner?"

"Of course," she said, unsure that she had prepared enough food for four people. "You two must be awfully tired after such a long trip."

"Yeah, we sure are. A hot bath would be nice too, wouldn't it, Honey."

"Sure would, Sweetheart. And a good nights sleep."

"Well, put your bags in the spare bedroom. After dinner, I'll heat some water and you two can have a good hot bath. How does that sound?"

"Awfully good, don't it, Honey!"

A few minutes later the front door opened and Walter walked in, shocked to see the couple. Raymond stepped forward tentatively to greet his father. "Hi, Pap, we just got in from the bus station a little while ago."

June noticed that even though he had been gone for almost a year, he didn't hug his father. She and Raymond had talked a lot about their families on the train ride to Knoxville and she picked up on the fact that his father was not inclined toward affection, cordiality or the finer points of conversation.

Walter set down his lunch pail and looked the two of them up and down.

June moved beside her husband. "Hello, Mr. Bledsoe. My name is June. I'm glad to meet you." She stuck out her hand. "Raymond has told me a lot about you."

Walter only nodded toward his son. "Are you his girlfriend?"

"No, Mr. Bledsoe, I'm his wife."

Walter looked at June as if she had lost her mind; then he glowered at Raymond as if he was a damn fool.

Just then Mary brought a plate of fried chicken and a basket of biscuits from the kitchen and set them on the table. She said, "Dinner is ready." She nodded at the couple and then Walter, "Why don't you wash your hands, then Raymond and June can tell us about their trip while we're eating."

Raymond motioned to June, "Come on, Honey, let's wash up." He pointed toward the bedroom. "The bathroom's in there."

When they were in the bathroom, June whispered to Raymond, "He ain't very friendly is he!"

"No. Pap's not a big talker. He's serious most of the time. My brother used to warn me that Pap doesn't take well to surprises. But don't worry. He'll loosen up once he gets to know you."

Meanwhile in the kitchen Walter had a scowl on his face. "Where the hell did he find her?" he groused to Mary.

"They met in Cincinnati day before yesterday. You can tell they love one another a lot."

"They've known each other for two days, and they're madly in love. Sometimes I wonder what that boy has for brains!"

"Walter, he's a grown man and that woman is his wife. Let's have dinner and get to know her before we judge her—or your son."

After Walter had washed his hands, they sat down to eat. When they were all served, Raymond said, "Say, Pap, can we stay in the spare bedroom for a few days while I look for a job? June has offered to help Mama with the chores."

"In other words, Son, you're broke. Is that what you mean?"

"Yeah, I'm just about broke, Pap. The Navy doesn't pay a seaman much. I had to spend most of my severance pay just traveling to get here from San Francisco."

Walter regarded his son straight on. "Well, if this woman is really your wife, you'd better find a job fast so you can support her."

"I know that, Pap. I thought I would talk to Henry at Molyneux. He liked Kenneth and Kenneth always said he was a good boss. Besides, I bet he would sell me one of his old Chevys cheap. I'm going to put in an application at the knitting mill and the iron works too."

Walter clenched his jaw and glared at his son. "Raymond, the problem is there's a whole lot of other fellers coming home from the war now and they're lookin' for jobs too. Since you don't have a job, this probably wasn't a good time to take on a family."

"Pap, I can't help that. I do love June and we are married."

June was fuming, on the verge of losing her temper. Finally, she stood up, unable to hold back any longer. "Wait a minute, Mister Bledsoe, whether you like it or not, I am his wife. And he asked you a question: if we could stay here for a few days. If it's not asking too much, we need an answer. I know you've lost one son, but if you don't have the decency to help your other son, we'll go somewhere else and you can go to hell!"

Raymond became flustered and Mary was on the verge of tears. "Walter, we can't turn away our son and his wife," she pleaded. "For God's sake, why can't they stay here?"

"Pap, don't be upset at June. She's just worried about what we're gonna' do. I love her and I'm going to take care of her and our baby. I'm just askin' for a few days until we can get on our feet . . ."

Walter's eyes grew wide in surprise. "Did you say *baby*?"

"Yes, Pap, June has a baby boy, two years old. Sammy's his name. June's mother is keeping him until we can go to Harlan and bring him back with us."

"You married a woman with a baby by some other man, a woman you just met! What the hell is wrong with you, boy?"

"Yes, I did, Pap. I did because I love June and me and her are going to raise that baby."

Mary's eyes opened wide and her face flushed. "You have a baby!"

"Yes, Mom. I do. He's a good lookin' baby. A smart baby too."

"Whoa now!" Walter shouted at June in disbelief. "What about the father?"

"What about him?" she shot back at him. She was furious and she wasn't going to let anybody browbeat her.

"I mean where is he? Were you married to him?" Walter pressed, his voice taking on a harsh edge.

"How should I know where he is?" June shot back. "He was abusive so I left his sorry ass. We were only together six months."

Walter regarded Raymond sternly. "Raymond, if you're really married to this woman, you can't stay here. You can't bring a stranger into this house."

Raymond sighed and stared at the floor, feeling humiliated and unsure. He looked up at his father, his eyes pleading. "Pap, I have only $27.00 left to carry us through until I get a job. I don't know where else we can go."

Walter was unmoved. "Raymond, did you hear what I said? if you're a married man, you're gonna' have to act like one. You're gonna' have to support her. It ain't my place to handle your problems now."

Mary was horrified, unable to utter a word.

June's mouth dropped in disbelief. Now she felt humiliated, treated like trash.

Raymond said, "Pap, I am gonna' support her. I just need a little time to find a job . . . And we don't have any place to go."

Mary gingerly touched Walter's arm, "Walter, please . . ."

Walter gave his son a withering look. "All right, you can stay here for a week or two while you look for a job. But you sure as hell can't bring a baby in here, crying and waking us up."

"Okay, Pap, we'll take you up on your offer since we don't have anywhere else to go. Once we get Sammy, we won't bother you anymore."

Walter grunted, stomped into his bedroom and shut the door.

Raymond turned to June. "If you don't mind staying here until I get paid, then we can rent a room at the motor court until we can get our own place. Then we can go to Harlan and pick up Sammy."

June stared at Raymond and shook her head. "I don't feel welcome here but I don't see where we have any choice." She turned away and walked outside. *I've made an awful mistake. This ain't gonna' work*, she thought. She sat down on the porch steps and started to cry.

Mary went out on the porch to assuage June's hurt feelings. "He's not as bad as he sounds. Why don't you take a warm bath? You'll feel a lot better and you can get a good night's sleep. I'll fix you a tub of warm water. Okay?"

June wiped the tears from her eyes. "Okay, thanks."

"I'll fill you a tub out on the back porch where you can have some privacy."

After June and Raymond had both bathed in his parent's big galvanized tub, they felt much better. They went into the spare bedroom and laid down on the bed. "What are you gonna' do tomorrow?" she asked.

"After I get a good nights sleep, I'm gonna' hitchhike into town and see if I can find a job. I'll get Mom to pack me a lunch and some coffee. Pap goes to work about seven. You can sleep in as long as you want. Then you and Mom can get acquainted. She's a gem; she'll fix you some breakfast and show you around. Maybe you can help her with some of the chores."

"Okay, but I don't think your father is ever gonna' like me."

Raymond leaned over and kissed her. "Don't worry. He don't hardly like anybody. He's awful pigheaded— and suspicious—but once he gets to know you, he'll be nice to you."

They kissed again and fell into a heavy sleep. When they awoke the next morning, it was almost 10:00 and the sun was shining brightly. "You two look a sight better," Mary said. "How 'bout some bacon and eggs and a cup of coffee?"

When Raymond returned that afternoon, he had found a job at the Rockwood Iron Works Company making $1.25/hour for collecting the pig iron from the blast furnaces and transporting it to the loading docks for shipping.

June was missing her baby and, now that Raymond had a job, she was anxious to have Sammy with her. And she was eager for Raymond to see *their* baby. She was also hopeful that when Walter saw how little trouble Sammy was and how cute he looked that he would welcome her and Sammy into the family. Mary did quickly accept her and was eager to help the newly weds anyway she could.

June also hoped that Walter would relent and allow them to stay a few more weeks so they could save up some money for a down payment on a small house of their own and a used car. For the next two weeks, however, Walter mostly ignored her and said little to Raymond, making it obvious he considered them an imposition.

When Raymond received his first paycheck, it was for $85.00 for two weeks work. He gave his mother $15.00 to help with the groceries; she refused to accept the money at first but he insisted.

Raymond took $50.00 and put it down on a 1939 four-door Chevy Sedan in good condition that he bought for $375.00. That only left them $20.00 to get by on for two weeks, but he knew a car would make it easier to get to and from work and would help make a good impression on June's parents.

He and June also figured they could save money by driving to Harlan instead of taking the bus since that would be cheaper than buying two roundtrip bus tickets. Gasoline cost about 20 cents per gallon so the 230 mile round trip would cost only about $3.50. And they would feel that their family was making progress.

The next weekend they drove up to Harlan, arriving late on a Saturday afternoon. John was not yet home from work, but June's two younger sisters Ruth and Mattie Lee were playing in the yard behind the house.

June pushed open the front door and yelled, "Mommy, it's June. I'm home." Mattie and Ruth, carrying Sammy, came running. Both of them were skinny as fence posts, but Ruth was 13 and stout enough to carry Sammy on her hip. They were thrilled to see June. First June picked up Sammy and hugged him tightly and then she hugged her little sisters as Rhoda appeared. "Mommy, this is my husband Raymond," she beamed. "We were married about a month ago."

June turned to Raymond and gestured toward her mother. "This is my mother, Rhoda."

Raymond said, "I'm pleased to meet you, Mrs. Brittian."

Rhoda nodded and invited them in out of the cold.

June gestured toward Sammy and said to Raymond, "And this here is my baby Sammy. See what a good baby he is." Sammy smiled and June handed him to Raymond who was not sure what to do.

When John came home, they sat around the dinner table and talked until late in the night. It was the first time June had felt complete; at last she was part of a happy family. Sunday morning after breakfast and before Rhoda had to be at church, they loaded the old Chevrolet with their few belongings and headed back to Rockwood.

June and Raymond were pleased about the warm welcome they had received from her parents and they were hopeful of an equally warm reception from Walter when he saw their baby. For the first time they felt optimistic about their future prospects.

When they arrived at his parent's home, it was late in the afternoon on Sunday. Walter was sitting on the porch smoking a pipe. When they got out of the car and he saw June was carrying Sammy, a frown came over his face.

"Hello, Mr. Bledsoe," June said uneasily, stepping up on the porch. Walter just glared at her.

"Hey, Pap, look here who we've got!" Raymond said as he gestured toward Sammy.

Walter ignored June and stood up to face his son. "Raymond, why are you bringing that woman AND her baby here?" he growled through clenched teeth. "I told you not to do that."

Raymond froze, at a loss for words. June stepped back, holding Sammy tighter. *How stupid of me to think that old goat might change his mind*, she fumed.

"Pap, we just need a place to stay until we can get a place of our own. We thought you might change your mind when you saw what a good baby Sammy is. He won't be no trouble, Pap, he hardly ever cries."

"Damn it, Boy, I meant what I said. This is my house and there ain't going to be no baby in this house."

"Pap, I wish you wouldn't call me 'Boy'. I'm a grown man, married and old enough to serve in the Navy."

"I'll be glad to do that, Son, when you start actin' like a man."

Raymond was floored—it was like watching the beginning of a train wreck and he had no idea how to stop it.

Nor was it the homecoming June had expected. "You're a hateful ol' son of a bitch," she yelled at Walter. "I hope you rot in hell!" She spun around, stormed off the porch and deposited Sammy in their car.

Mary heard the commotion and rushed out onto the porch. When she saw June and heard the baby crying, she threw up her hands. "Walter, for God's sake, why can't we help them? We can't turn our only son's family away."

Walter's face was red and his tone was threatening. "Shut up and get back in the house," he ordered. Humiliated, Mary retreated just inside the screen door.

"You can't stay here with that baby," Walter repeated more firmly to Raymond.

June stormed back to the porch, clenching her fists, and confronted Walter. "Your son is a better man than you'll ever be, you cold-hearted old bastard," she shouted at him.

Walter made a threatening move toward her as if he were going to slap her.

June was defiant and refused to back up an inch. "You touch me and I'll scratch your eyes out, you miserable old . . ."

Raymond watched in horror as his wife and father almost came to blows. She stopped in mid sentence and turned to Raymond. "Come on, we're not wanted here. We'll sleep in the car if we have to."

June glimpsed Mary, clearly distraught, watching them leave and realized how terrible the poor woman felt. June shouted to her, "Don't worry. We'll be all right."

Raymond said, "I'm sorry, honey." He put his arm around June's shoulder and opened the car door. "I've got an idea," he said. We'll go to Mom's family, the Fullers. Pap doesn't have anything to do with them—I don't know why—but they'll let us spend the night. We'll tell them what happened. They'll understand."

There were tears in her eyes but she nodded her approval. June was hurt so deeply and so full of a silent rage she could hardly breathe.

They drove the half mile to the Fuller house. When they arrived, Mary's parents, Johnce and Emma Fuller, were getting ready to sit down to dinner. When Raymond explained the situation to them, Johnce shook his head and sighed. "Of course, you can stay here. We're just getting ready to have dinner. Please join us."

Johnce turned to June, "You and your baby are welcome here. We're glad to have you."

Raymond's aunts, Reba and Elizabeth, who had never married and continued to live with their parents, joined them. While they were eating, Grandma Fuller said to Raymond, "Your father has always been difficult to get along with. Over the years, we've been concerned about your mother being mistreated. I've always thought your father was too harsh with her and too hard on you boys. We hear he drinks too much and is mean when he's drunk. Oh, she never complains, but we know Walter's hard to live with. He doesn't seem to like us or want to be around us, although we've always tried to make him feel welcome."

Johnce said to June, "To be treated the way you were by your father-in-law was hurtful, I know. But Emma's right; that's just his nature. I'm sorry. But if we can help you, we will. If I can put in a good word for Raymond to help him get a decent job, I'll be happy to do that if the job he has now doesn't work out."

The Fullers didn't have a spare bedroom and Raymond didn't want to impose on them by staying more than a couple of days. Nor did he have enough money to rent a room at the travel court that was across the road, so they slept on the floor. The next day he drove to Harriman after work and bought a surplus Army tent. It would have to do for a few days until he could figure out a permanent housing arrangement.

Wednesday after work, Raymond pitched the tent in a lightly wooded area close to his parent's house. For the next few weeks, he and June would take a sponge bath from a pan of water. On weekends, usually early on a Saturday, they would take a real bath in the tub he borrowed from his mother who left it for him on the porch. Often Mary would cook extra food for dinner and take it to June before the men got home from work.

Around this time, for some unknown reason, June decided to take on a new name. She decided she wanted to be called "Terrie" and she encouraged Raymond and her extended family to call her "Terrie", although some of her friends continued to call her "June" out of habit. She never explained the change to her children and they never thought to ask her.

Rockwood didn't have the damp and biting chill that Harlan had in winter, but June was not happy living in a tent with no amenities while trying to care for a baby. Eastern Tennessee was still plenty cold in March. Once when they were huddled together to stay warm, June put her hand on a snake under the covers with them. After that, it was hard for Raymond to convince her that things would get better. Sometimes when Walter was drinking and it was not wise to come around, they would scrape together a few dollars and spend a night in one of the travel lodge units so they could clean up and get a good night's rest.

This sequence would continue for the next six months until June and Raymond had saved enough money for the first month's rent on a small house in Midtown. Raymond had gotten a job at the hosiery mill in Harriman where his father worked. Sometimes Mary would take the bus to visit them on the weekend and bring them a dish for dinner or something canned from the garden.

After almost three years in Midtown, June and Raymond decided to move to a small rental house in Pond Grove, about a mile from the Rockwood city limits. He worked out a transfer from the mill in Harriman to the one in Rockwood and was able to save money by riding a bicycle back and forth to work. Furthermore, Sammy would be beginning first grade in the fall and they would be close to the small elementary school he would be attending in the Pond Grove community. Furthermore, the uneasy relationship between Raymond and his father had eventually improved and he wanted to be closer to his parents.

In the fall June found out that she was pregnant and on May 8, 1950, she gave birth to a baby boy named Kenneth Ray. The new baby smiled a lot and seemed so happy that his proud parents nicknamed him "Smiley". In the summer of 1951, June learned that she was again pregnant and in 1952, she delivered a beautiful baby girl Pamella June.

In the early years of their marriage, it was hard to make ends meet. For much of that time Raymond was unemployed. Like his father, he was a hard worker with a talent for fixing mechanical things. But the following year America slid into a recession that lasted from 1953 until the end of 1955. Raymond was out of work for all three of those years.

Using his VA entitlement, in 1957 he completed the training needed to join the union and get a good job at the government's nuclear facility in Oak Ridge. From then until he retired, he worked as a plumber-steam fitter in the pipefitting industry. That job relieved the financial stress they had suffered in the early years of their marriage.

In 1956, President Dwight Eisenhower signed the Federal-Aid Highway Act that authorized the construction of a nationwide expressway system that would benefit the country in many ways. The new interstate highways were controlled-access expressways with no at-grade crossings—that is, they had overpasses and underpasses instead of intersections. They were at least four lanes wide and were designed for high-speed driving.

The bill created a 41,000-mile national system of "Interstate and Defense Highways" intended to eliminate traffic congestion, replace "undesirable slum areas", and make coast-to-coast transportation safer and more efficient.

World War II was over but the Cold War tensions between Russia and America were ratcheting up; the new system would make it easy to get out of big cities in case of an atomic attack. But more importantly for those who were struggling to make ends meet, a major benefit was the creation of jobs that would help lift the country out of the recession.

The poisoned relationship between Raymond's father and June never became cordial and his father never developed a close relationship with his three grandchildren. Walter was an avid fisherman but he took Sammy fishing only once. Even though Raymond and his family lived directly across the road from his parents on Highway 70, Walter rarely visited them and made no effort to become a part of their lives in any way.

Raymond's mother did enjoy a close relationship with her three grandchildren, however, and she walked with them to the small Post Oak Christian Church almost every Sunday.

As a critical part of the war effort, Oak Ridge was secretly built to develop the atomic bomb. During the 50s, Raymond trained and qualified as a welder. His skills enabled him to eventually qualify for a job at the Y-12 government plant in Oak Ridge as a pipe fitter making significantly more money. The couple decided they could finally afford a house of their own if Raymond could build much of it himself.

He eagerly took on the task and did much of the carpentry, masonry and plumbing himself. In 1958, they moved into their new brick home on a lot straight across the highway from his parents. At last one of June's dreams was fulfilled. She had a nice home with a modern kitchen. The house was on seven hilly acres surrounded by oaks, pines, persimmon trees, dogwoods and poplars. It was a huge step up from the log cabin she had occupied for several years while growing up.

If there was one thing Raymond excelled at, it was gardening. He had a talent for growing things. He had apple trees, pear trees, persimmon trees and grapevines. He also kept honey bees for a few years.

There was a good place for a sizeable garden and the soil was rich so he tried his hand at raising a variety of vegetables. He raised different crops from year to year, including, corn, potatoes, radishes, green beans, peas, okra, peanuts, cucumbers, water melons, onions, cabbage, strawberries and hay. In her younger years, June canned a fair amount of that produce. In the late 50s when he bought a small Farmall tractor, his gardens became even bigger.

Raymond had another good quality: he never drank. Although his father Walter was an alcoholic, Raymond never took up the habit. Nor did he smoke.

June and Raymond were doing better financially, but there were problems brewing at home. Raymond was not organized and he never threw anything away. In other words, he was a hoarder so that became a source of friction between them.

Raymond was at work and the children were in school during the week so June was by herself a lot. On the weekends, weather permitting, Raymond worked in his garden unless he was working on building a barn or some other kind of outbuilding. During the spring and summers, he often came in from the garden or lawn soaked in sweat.

June was not happy and they often argued. She was always swamped with chores: cooking, cleaning, canning, doing laundry and caring for three children. There was no opportunity for a social life, but Raymond wasn't interested in socializing anyway. They never went to a movie, ate out at a restaurant, or took a vacation.

She was happiest when they went away for the weekend to visit her relatives in Kentucky or Alabama. She loved to listen to music, to sing, and to dance. But Raymond never made time for such things. So June felt trapped in a tedious and contentious marriage.

In those days the local church offered the best chance to meet other people and socialize. But Raymond did not grow up inclined to socialize or attend church, even though his mother was a devout Christian and faithful in her attendance.

Nor was June inclined to attend church. She had been frightened and turned off by her mother's shenanigans in the small fundamentalist church where they handled snakes, shouted gibberish, and handled hot coals.

Mary did take the three children to church with her often when they were old enough to make the mile long walk to her small country church. But Raymond and June rarely attended church.

In 1953, there was a crisis so serious that June believed she had no recourse but to leave and seek a divorce. She left Raymond and the children and returned temporarily to her parent's home in Harlan until she could figure out what to do. Both of them had insecurities carried over from their childhoods and both of them were flirtatious and jealous. She contacted a divorce lawyer in Louisville, Kentucky where she hoped to start a new life. But, desperately missing her children, she began attempts to reconcile their differences. Using her common name "Terrie", she wrote the attached letter to her estranged husband, expressing so poignantly the hurt and despair she felt.

March 1, 1954

Dear Raymond & Children,

Last night when you called me you was plenty sore and I don't blame you. But Raymond what you didn't let me tell you was why I was so worried. Honey I've nearly been crazy thinking about my children. Honey, if you'll please forgive me for doing this to you & children, I promise long as I live I'll never go any place without you or them. I know I was wrong in coming up here. Mommy didn't need me half as much as my little children needed me. Honey I swear I'm sorry from the very bottom of my heart. I've been a fool but not any more. Will you Dear let me try to make up for the way I left you & them. I'm sorry. I want to show you that I am. I'll prove it Honey, I swear it. Raymond, if you won't forgive my leaving like I did & never remind me of it anymore, I'll come back & show you just how sorry I am. But other wise I won't come back. Let me know soon as possible how you feel about this.

All my love, Terrie

Dear please don't mistrust me so much. I have no intention of being untrue to you till you say we're through. So Bye Bye, Love always

Sammy x x x x x x x x x x

Smiley x x x x x x x x x x

Pamella x x x x x x x x x x

Raymond x x x x x x x x x

There's a six inch snow on up here now. Weather is freezing me to death.

But they were not able to overcome their problems and their marriage continued to founder, leading to further separation. In 1955, June wrote the following letter revealing her confusion and despair:

By the time you read this, I'll be far away, out of your life, the wife you hate to come home to. Goodbye.

Dearest Raymond,

I'm so sorry to have to do this and I don't how how I'll ever live over it. But the time has come when I can't bear this hurt any longer. You'll never know till you have the same feeling just how you've hurt me. What hurts most is I don't know what has brought this on. I guess I knew long ago it'd happen sooner or later. But why if you knew did you let me stay all this time and waste so many years of my life? The sad part is I just don't care anymore. I've lost my pride which is all I had to hang onto. Whatever you decide, please don't take the children or the house from me. If you try to, I don't think God would ever forgive you for it. All I ask is please take care of the kids, especially Sammy. He has no one but me and nobody can ever take him from me. Raymond, do what you think best . . . live a rough life if you want to for you're the one who will have to answer & live with yourself. I'm even sorry for myself because it looks like it was never meant for me to ever have happiness. I'll pray for you and wish you the best of everything. Someday you'll wake up and find out what a mistake you've made by hurting me so. I've done the very best I could but someone else has lured you away. But they're friends that will soon go their way. Please look after Sam for me & Smiley & Pamella. If I find a job, I'll try to make arrangements to have them with me. Please don't call or write. As always Devoted, Terrie

(early 1955)

After several months apart, they reconciled, mostly it appears for the sake of their children. But problems lingered. As their children grew up and moved on with their lives, June and Raymond's marriage, suffering from vague ongoing infidelities, remained stormy and uncertain. The two of them were different in many ways.

They were alike in that they were both kind-hearted and congenial with a robust sense of humor but they also had vicious and fiery tempers. From time to time they had fierce fights. When they were aroused to anger, neither one of them tended to hold back. No matter what difficulties they faced, however, they never took their frustrations and anger out on their children and always remained kind and loving parents.

June loved to socialize with friends but, not going to church, she had few opportunities to make friends. She loved to dance too, although she only got to dance with Sammy a hand full of times on special occasions like her birthday after he was grown. She loved music. She was a true romantic at heart and a heartfelt romantic song could make her cry. One of her favorites and a song that always made her cry was **Hero**, sung by *Enrique Iglesias*.

Eventually all three children returned to east Tennessee and remained close to their parents for the rest of their lives. Joining their parents for Sunday lunch was a cherished tradition

When Sammy graduated from High School in 1962, he joined the Naval ROTC program at the University of North Carolina. Upon graduation in 1966, he began four years of active duty as an officer in the Navy. He was the first child in his parent's or his grandparent's generation to attend college. He also married his high school sweetheart that year, and they had one daughter. After completing his military service, he returned to Tennessee to work in Chattanooga as an insurance agent. He was eventually promoted to General Agent for a major life insurance company in Lexington, Kentucky. He continued to work in sales until he retired.

After Ken graduated from high school in 1969, he enlisted in the Marine Corps for three years and received orders to Parris Island, South Carolina for basic training. After completing his training there, he continued his training in Jacksonville, North Carolina and then at Camp Pendleton, just north of San Diego, before serving in Vietnam for two years in artillery. He married in 1971, divorced in 1972 and remarried in 1980. Throughout his married life, he lived and worked in the Knoxville area.

Ken was a lot like his father—kind-hearted and generous to a fault with a friendly disposition. He was also mechanically inclined, able to fix almost anything, whether a tractor or a lawnmower, and a hard worker. thletic

After Pam graduated from high school in 1970, she took business courses at a business college in Knoxville and then took a job with the state Department of Human Services. She married in 1972 and lived in Kingston, close to her parents. From their 70s until the last years of her parent's lives, she took responsibility for looking after them and too often had to mediate between them when they were quarreling.

When June and Raymond reached their early 80s, they both began to develop dementia. As the disease progressed, the strain, especially on Pam as their caregiver, became hard to bear but she never complained. On October 18, 2014 Raymond died at home. On March 23, 2016, June passed away in a nursing home at the age of 91.

JUNE AND RAYMOND WITH ALL THREE CHILDREN

Pamella June — Born 1954   Kenneth Ray — Born 1952

Delores

Like her sister June, Mary Ruth Brittian was born in a log cabin in Gray's Knob, not much more than a wide spot in the road in eastern Kentucky, the sixth of seven children, on June 15, 1932. She arrived seven years after her older sister June was born. Ruth was mature for her age and strong willed, not submissive like girls were expected to be in those days. Although there was a significant age difference between the two, Ruth and June were always close.

Like her older sister, Ruth was stubborn and didn't get along well with her mother. By the time she was eight years old, her mother required her to take on some of the responsibilities for cooking and cleaning at home. Like the other Brittian children, she didn't get much schooling. Sometimes when she came home from school desperately hungry, her mother would be engrossed in her Bible study, sometimes with neighborhood ladies, seemingly unaware that there wasn't anything to eat.

Her parents didn't much care whether she went to school or not. They were too busy with their own problems just making ends meet. Without much parental involvement in her life, Ruth was left to figure out how things worked on her own. Like her older sister, she yearned for the love, stability and security that was missing from her childhood. As a result, she learned to be cynical and untrusting. It seemed that Ruth and June were always in trouble with their mother.

There were some things you could say about the Brittian girls that were beyond dispute: they had guts, they were independent and they had a temper. Although they were kind hearted with a rather dry sense of humor, they were inclined to verbally flay you alive if you crossed them. When they set out alone into the world to escape the grinding poverty of eastern Kentucky, they were not shy about asking for help. And they didn't shy away from standing up for themselves.

Growing up as a young woman in a man's world was not easy, especially if you were poor and uneducated. Ruth quickly learned that men made almost all of the decisions, enjoyed more freedom and had far more opportunities than women. Observing the hard life that her father had, however, she realized life could also be hard for men who were poor and uneducated.

When Ruth was a teenager, Rhoda sometimes took her and her sister Mattie Lee to visit their Aunt Mary in Lynchburg, Virginia. Rhoda and Mary were infatuated by the female Holiness evangelist Effie Gilmer who traveled around Virginia and Kentucky preaching at revivals that often lasted several days. Usually Rhoda took Ruth and Mattie with her to stay at Mary's and the girls went with their mother and aunt to all of the revival services. Rhoda never learned to drive so Mary's son Sam Brown drove over and picked them up. When the girls were a little older, Rhoda left the girls with their father and went to stay with her sister Mary in Virginia for as long as a month at a time.

Mary worked in a dry cleaning business and Rhoda helped her by washing and pressing clothes and doing some cooking to cover their room and board at Mary's. Mary was divorced from her first husband Joe Brown who had fathered four children with her.

One of those children was Sam Brown who, although he was married with several children, secretly abused Ruth by trying to touch her in inappropriate places. Such behavior infuriated and disgusted Ruth and made her desperate to leave. When she complained to her mother about her cousin's behavior, her mother scolded her and told her to ignore the situation to avoid an uncomfortable confrontation.

Ruth and Mattie were always on their own while their mother worked. It was late in the summer and they were out of school so they wandered around neighboring fields and gathered wild apples, paw paws, walnuts, blackberries and muscadine grapes when they found them.

Ruth was bored and unhappy with her situation when they were at Mary's. She was eager to be grown up and get a job. While wandering in the fields across a hill near Mary's house, Ruth and Mattie saw a manufacturing plant in the distance.

Ruth gazed at the plant and imagined what it would be like to work there. She decided to go and see for herself. She pointed Mattie back toward Aunt Mary's and warned her, "Don't you tell Momma where I'm going. It's our secret. Okay?" Mattie nodded okay and Ruth began the long walk to the plant which was at least a mile away. When she arrived, she asked the receptionist whom she could talk to about a job.

The receptionist studied her for a minute and then smiled. "Well, I suppose Mr. Hines could talk to you if he's not too busy. What's your name?"

"Ruth Brittian."

"Well, my name is Evelyn." She winked at Ruth, "Wait here," and disappeared through the door behind her desk.

A few minutes later, a tall man with bright brown eyes, a mustache and rolled up shirt sleeves appeared. "Hello, I'm Mr. Hines. Miss Carter tells me you're looking for a job."

"Yes, sir, I am," Ruth replied.

Mr. Hines looked her up and down. "How old are you?" he asked.

She lowered her gaze. "I'm 18, sir," she replied, a little nervously. He studied her for a minute and frowned. "You're not 18."

Ruth didn't hesitate. "Well, I need a job," she replied firmly with a hint of desperation in her voice.

He was taken aback, impressed by her force of will. She was a mere child but there was something about her that made her seem mature beyond her years. He was a man of discipline and order, an honest man who followed the rules. Obviously, the impish girl before him was too young to legally hire. It would be foolish to consider such a thing.

But there was something captivating about her. She needed help. He sensed it and he could not, indeed he would not, allow himself to dismiss her. He thought of his own daughter who was about this girl's age. He set his mind to work, considering the possibilities.

The answer came in a flash of inspiration that pleased him. He smiled down at Ruth. "Maybe I can find something for you to do. Come with me."

On the second floor of the factory, there were four monstrous machines that spit out long continuous sheets of wide colored fabric that were rolled on to hard paper cores. "Look here," Mr. Hines said as he pointed to the large rolls of fabric. "I can hire you to look after these rolls to make sure the fabric doesn't go off center and bunch up on these rolls. If the fabric starts to bunch up and we don't stop the machines immediately, it's costly and a lot of trouble to straighten out the fabric. We can't ship it out to our customers if it's crooked on the rolls. So, you can be our quality control person."

He pointed to a large lever at the end of each of the machines. "You have to pull back hard on that lever to stop the machine as soon as you see the fabric becoming crooked or bunched up. An alarm will go off and the foreman will come to straighten the fabric. Can you do that?"

"Yes, Sir, I can," she replied.

"All right," he said. "You can start tomorrow morning. Be here at 8:00. Bring your lunch. Quitting time is 5:00. You'll work Monday through Saturday." He smiled at her: "Any questions?"

Her heart was racing. She couldn't believe her ears. "No, Sir. Thank you, Sir."

When she got home, her mother was still at work but Mattie Lee was waiting for her on the steps to the old house. She puffed out her chest and proudly announced, "Mattie, I got myself a job. I'll be going to work everyday just like Mommy."

Mattie giggled and hugged her sister. "Mommy will be proud of you. Can I go to work with you?"

"No, you can't go to work with me. I'll be too busy. And I'm not going to tell Mommy about it. She'll just get mad at me and say I'm not old enough to have a job. And you can't tell her either. It's our secret."

"Okay," Mattie replied, "but what will I do all day?"

"Just stay here and play with your doll. When I get home, I'll tell you all about my job. Just don't tell Mommy." Ruth wasn't worried about Mattie spilling the beans because Mattie always covered up for her sister. If her mother questioned her about something Ruth had done, Mattie always feigned ignorance.

Ruth threw herself on her bed and thought about the big building, the huge machines, Evelyn and Mr. Hines. They were both kind to her. She was proud of herself for getting a job but she was nervous about her first day. She would have to pack a modest lunch—an apple and a bacon and fried egg sandwich would do just fine—and leave at 7:30 the next morning—about the same time her mother left with her aunt. Then there was the church service or revival she would have to attend with her mother and aunt in the evenings.

Her first day on the job went well and she got to talk to Evelyn and Mr. Hines and meet some of the other employees. But after her fourth day on the job, her mother told her it was time for them to go home. Ruth had worked at the plant for one week and earned $38.00. When she informed Mr. Hines that she had to give up her job and go back to Kentucky, he said he was sorry to see her go. She thanked him and hugged Evelyn. She asked to be paid in cash. It was like a fortune to her; she clutched the money tightly in her hand, afraid to trust it to the safe keeping of her pocket, as she walked the long way home.

Soon after Rhoda and her two girls reached their home, she sent Ruth to keep house for her great uncle "Will" Smith and his wife Sarah. Uncle Will was in his seventies and Sarah was blind. They paid Ruth $2.00 per week for doing chores around the house.

Ruth didn't mind helping them out and she was glad to earn a little bit of money although she got to keep very little of it. Besides that, it was good to escape the harsh and chaotic conditions within the Brittian household that were primarily caused by her mother's neglect and her brother Jay's bullying.

After a few months, all of that changed for the worse, however. Uncle Will couldn't help but notice that Ruth was becoming more mature and developing small breasts. When he became too "familiar" with her, she became upset and complained to her mother. But her mother would have none of that; she only scolded Ruth and made her cry for even bringing it up. "Don't you be saying things like that," she chastened. "You don't know what you're talking about." That was the last straw. Ruth made up her mind that she wasn't going to stay there any longer.

She felt stifled in Harlan County and the last thing she intended to do was wind up a coal miner's wife in eastern Kentucky like her mother. Her sister June had left home several years before and Ruth was anxious to go out on her own. She had learned a lot by listening to the stories June told about her experiences while on her own. And there were things she had learned from her brief job experience. She realized there were a few good men like Harvey Perkins with his chicken coop and Mr. Hines out there in the world who would help you. And something else: *If you need help, you have got to ask for it—and never be afraid to speak up.* Beyond that, she had gained a lot of confidence that led her to believe she could make it on her own.

There was one bright spot in Ruth's life. When June was 19 and had her baby, Sammy, Ruth was only 12 years old. By the time Sammy was six months old, June had to hustle to find either a job or a husband. She didn't want to leave but she had no choice, even though she was uneasy about the care her baby would receive since her parents were getting older.

Ruth, although a mere child herself, took up the slack and by the age of 13 both she and the baby had bonded and Ruth became Sammy's surrogate mother. June was gone a lot trying to find a stable life, and for the next few years in June's absence Ruth helped raise her baby nephew. When Ruth was away at school, Sammy would eagerly watch for her from the front porch. When he spotted her coming up the path, he would yell, "Hey, Ru'", then run to her and jump into her arms. She would carry him to the porch on her hip. Those were some of the happiest times of her young years. Throughout her life she would recall with a smile how she hauled her young nephew around like a sack of potatoes.

As Ruth became more mature, everyone who met her agreed that she was beautiful. She had a smooth, sultry voice that pleased like a sip of cold Kentucky bourbon on a hot summer day. Her personality, so warm and inviting, drew men to her like bears to honey.

Ruth had little money but she knew how to dress well. She was not educated but she quickly learned how to get by. As a teenager, she had heard June's sad stories of how men could use you and break your heart. She became convinced that most men were not to be trusted. She made up her mind that no man was going to take advantage of her and hurt her the way her sister had been treated. So, when she was on her own, she was was determined that she would not be exploited or controlled.

When Ruth was 16, she met Larry Lowe, a handsome fellow with bright blue eyes, wearing his Air Force uniform in the Corbin train station. He was from Pineville, about 30 miles up the road from Williamsburg and he was on his way back to the Lowry Field Air Force Base in Denver. He immediately fell madly in love with her. He delayed his departure so they could spent the day together. He promised he would write her and he did.

He also sent her $50 to cover her expenses so she could come to Denver to see him. But she didn't go. Inclined to be distrusting, she had sized up Larry as a fast talker and decided that nothing would come of their meeting so she simply ignored his letters and forgot about him. Besides, she could do a lot with $50. She kept the money and used it to buy two dresses.

A few weeks later she went to Norwood, Ohio, a suburb of Cincinnati, to work. She and Clara Lawson, a friend of hers from Williamsburg, had a small sleeping room—it wasn't much—with a little place to heat coffee.

When Delores met Larry, she had pretty long hair—that's how he remembered her. At 7:00 one morning there was a knock on the door. To her shock, Larry was standing there. "What in the hell happened to you!" he exclaimed, referring to her hair that was then short.

"Well, who the hell are you?" she replied.

He'd been on leave back in Kentucky and had gone to her parent's house; they told him where she was living. He said, "I'm that guy that sent you $50 so you could come and see him and you never showed up."

She played dumb. "I don't know anything about $50—if you sent it to me, I didn't get it!"

She finally let him in and he hung out with them all day. He bought them something to eat. They went to see the famous Tyler Fountain Square in bustling downtown Cincinnati and spent the day together. Out of the blue that evening at dinner he proposed to her. They had enjoyed a pleasant day together so she accepted. The next morning he had to catch the train back to Denver, but they agreed to marry as soon as they could get together again.

He said, "When I go on leave again, I'll come see you." When he returned several weeks later, they got married without ever going on a formal date. It was February 17, 1949; she had not yet turned 17.

After Larry got out of the Air Force, they moved to Ypsilanti, Michigan where the auto industry was booming. They both found jobs at auto plants there, Larry at the GM auto plant and Ruth at the Ford plant.

At this point in Ruth's story, some clarification is required. While married to Larry, she defiantly took control of her life and legally changed her name from Mary to Delores. From then on, she insisted that everyone call her "Delores".

She hated the name "Mary" because she was named after her aunt Mary whom she detested. Mary was overbearing and disdainful of the girls, making it clear she didn't want to be bothered with them.

Mary also behaved selfishly around them. Once when aunt Mary was visiting during the holidays, she brought a big bag of Christmas candy with her. She teased the girls by going around eating her candy in front of them but refusing to share it with them. She kept that candy to herself by storing it on a high shelf where Ruth and Mattie couldn't reach it. Small incidents like that fueled the girl's dislike for Mary and caused them to avoid her as much as they could.

Besides that, Ruth didn't like the name "Mary" because it was a biblical name. She didn't take to religion because her mother was so strict and hard on them. Ruth came to associate religion and "Church" with mean spirited people so she wanted no part of it.

Delores and Larry lived together for eleven years. They had been married about four years when Delores had their daughter Sandra Lynn who was born in Ypsilanti in 1954 when Delores was 22.

Delores' brother Sam used to come and stay with them from time to time. One year he talked Larry into quitting his job and taking off with him to Arizona. Sam had heard rumors there were good jobs there where you could make a lot of money. Both of them wound up in Grants, New Mexico and soon found jobs in the copper mines.

After a few paydays, Larry sent money to Delores and Sam sent money to his wife Jean so they could come to Grants. Taking her baby daughter and their meager belongings with her, Delores drove out to Grants to live. Jean came with them.

Delores had their second daugher Connie Bly in 1957 in San Manuel, Arizona. But Delores didn't like living in Arizona because the sand was everywhere; she would wake up in the morning and sand would have blown in under the door. And it was hot! Not long after Connie was born, Delores was ready to go back to Ypsilanti.

Delores had met Shirley Bennett, a young woman whose husband Wendell would beat her up. Shirley was fed up with her unhappy marriage and was also anxious to leave Grants. Delores didn't have enough money to get to her parent's home in Kentucky on her own. But Shirley had a little ol' 1954 blue Ford and she agreed to give Delores a ride to her parent's home in Harrisburg, Illinois. After Delores had rested up from their drive, Shirley's parents gave her money for a bus ticket to Williamsburg.

Eventually, Larry moved on to California looking for work and Delores, after leaving the girls with June and Raymond for the summer, followed him out to L.A.

One Saturday afternoon, after being together for a few months, Larry dropped her off at a grocery store and told her he was going to park the car. He never came back. He left her standing there and it started to rain. She was 28 and she had no money.

It was late at night and the store closed so she had to stand on the street. Finally a cab driver pulled over to the curb and asked her if she wanted a ride. She said no because she didn't have any money. The cab driver could see she was distressed and he was concerned about her. He came by several more times to check on her. It got dark and finally he came by with his taxi light off. He said, "You shouldn't be out here alone this late at night—I'll take you home or wherever you want to go."

Delores said she lived about ten miles away. He said, "I don't care where it is, I'll take you home. All you have to do is tell me where. It won't cost you a nickel." He took her back to the apartment she and Larry had.

The cabdriver said, "I'm going to wait and be sure you get in." She had no key so she had to wake up the landlady. When she came to the door, Delores told her she was locked out. After unlocking the door to her apartment, she returned the key to the thoroughly disgruntled landlady. She assured the cabdriver she was O.K. and thanked him. That's the last she saw of him but she never forgot his kindness.

Larry didn't come home until Tuesday. Delores realized then and there that their marriage was over. She suspected he had a date with someone else and he had decided to dump her.

She said, among other less charitable comments, "I only want one thing from you—I want a plane ticket back to Michigan and I want it this weekend." That was where Mattie and her husband Preston lived.

On her Thursday flight she had to change planes at Chicago O'Hare Airport. She went to the airline desk to inquire about her next flight. A guy at the ticket counter struck up a conversation with her and quickly offered to carry her bags to the other airline. By the time they reached the other airline ticket counter he had made a date with her, promising to come and see her in Detroit when he had a couple of days off.

She went to the waiting area and found a seat. When Thea F. Jones saw her walking across the floor in her white high heels, he exclaimed, "Lord, have mercy!" He ambled over and took a seat near her and struck up a conversation. He had on a pair of alligator dress shoes and wore an expensive suit and tie. He talked a little about politics and before long said, "It's been a long flight from Seattle and I'm thirsty. Where are you coming from?"

She said, "Los Angeles."

He said, "That's a long flight too. Would you like to go have a cold drink in the lounge?"

She said she would. They went to the lounge and continued their conversation. She told him she was flying to Detroit. He was flying to Philadelphia.

Soon it was time for him to catch his flight and they parted amicably. The last time she saw him he was running to catch his flight. Since her flight wouldn't leave for another hour, she went to the women's restroom but when she came back she was surprised: there he was on the phone and she noticed he had left his hat on the seat. She picked it up and walked over to him. She tapped him on the shoulder and said, "Here's your hat."

That pleased him greatly for he had already called her airline and bought a ticket so he could fly with her to Detroit. That was the beginning of their whirlwind romance. They walked around the airport; he said, "I've got a big blue Cadillac you'd really look good in."

She smiled and purred, "Really! Oh, I would like that."

He put his arm around her and, pulling her close, gave her a playful kiss. "This ain't gonna' end here," he breathed heavily.

He boarded the same flight she was on and talked one of the other passengers into switching seats with him so he could sit beside her. They got to know each other better and had a pleasant flight. When they landed in Detroit he met Mattie, Preston and Sandy. After a romantic dinner, he reluctantly flew on to Philadelphia. But come Monday he was back in Detroit after arranging for Preston to pick him up at the airport.

Perhaps the oddest thing about Delores and Philip's meeting was that they met at the Chicago O'Hare airport while he was flying from Seattle to Philadelphia and she was flying from L.A. to Detroit. Yet they both grew up poor, hardly more than a stones throw from each other in two small towns in Kentucky. He declared it was Karma; she said it was Fate.

Thea Felix Jones was born an only child to John A. and Arizona Jones, a poor family who lived in a log cabin in Williamsburg, Kentucky. He had a gift for talking and took up preaching as a young man. Later on, Delores was surprised to hear rumors that the father of her future husband had murdered a man and spent time in a Kentucky prison.

In 1960, Delores had an easy divorce from Larry. There were no assets to divide and no regrets. Four years later she and Thea were married in 1964. He bought her a nice brick rancher in Virginia Beach in Chesapeian Colony and helped her raise her two girls.

Delores had a thing for names. By then everyone was calling her by the nickname "Dee". She never liked the name Thea, so she took to calling him "Philip". He liked it.

Her husband was an outgoing and generous man, always upbeat and charismatic with a jovial sense of humor, but he was a mystery. For the first few years of their marriage, she never knew what he did for a living. He always flew to Philadelphia for long weekends of work and often traveled but he scrupulously evaded any questions about his vocation.

The mystery was finally solved when they were pulled over by a policeman one evening after a dinner in Philadelphia when Philip had drunk one scotch too many. The cop said "Good evening, Reverend Jones," and she finally realized to her surprise that he was a preacher and a famous one at that.

She eventually learned that he had become a minister and served in the Church Of God in Cleveland, Tennessee as a young man. In 1954, he bought the Metropolitan Opera House at Broad and Poplar streets in Philadelphia for $250,000 and hit the big time. Every Sunday 5,000 or more would pack the Met to hear him preach. Thousands tuned into his radio and television programs and attended his revival services as he traveled the country.

He was one of the first televangelists and TV personalities. Described as somewhere between evangelist Oral Roberts and Bishop Fulton Sheen, he had an easy going manner that carried a powerful message. He was also said to have the gift of healing the blind, deaf, lame and those suffering from other illnesses through prayer and oil anointing.

He didn't want his church to know about his private life because when he was at home in Virginia Beach, he never behaved like a preacher. He loved his scotch and he never prayed before meals. He loved to laugh and it may be that what his new family loved most about him was his sense of humor. You couldn't help but feel happier when you were around him.

Philip was a good stepfather to both girls and a mentor to Sandra since she was older. Philip was self-educated but articulate and well-informed. Sandra enjoyed the frequent talks they had about all manner of subjects including religion and philosophy. Since Larry made no effort to be a part of their lives, the girls soon thought of Philip as their actual father.

But Philip was 13 years older than Delores and she eventually tired of the long weekends apart. Losing patience with their living arrangement and feeling neglected, Delores was unhappy. Their marriage ended in divorce in 1974.

Soon after her divorce, she entered into a relationship with Bill Williford, a real estate investor in Virginia Beach, but it did not last long. There were relationships with several other men but she never found security or real happiness with any of them. Eventually she met retired Navy Chief Petty Officer Bill Mauk at the enlisted men's club on the Norfolk Navy Base. He was originally from Pennsylvania.

After marrying in 1980, they decided to move to Ypsilanti where the auto industry was hiring. They lived there for several years but Bill was in poor health and drank too much. He almost lost his job because of his drinking and in later years developed severe diabetes.

After he retired in 1999, Bill and Delores decided to swap the hard winters in Michigan for a rural lifestyle in Somerville, Alabama, near Huntsville. They bought a double wide mobile home and lived just across the country road from her sister Mattie and her husband Preston. But Bill's health continued to decline and in April of 2002, he passed away. He was a good husband who never hesitated to express his honest opinions.

About a year later she met Leo Lay in Atmore, Alabama where he had a winter home. Leo was a well-to-do farmer in Shippensburg, Pennsylvania. After they married, Leo sold his home in Atmore and Delores moved to Shippensburg where they lived together happily for several years until his death in 2014.

In 2017, Delores sold the house in Shippensburg and moved to South Carolina to live with her daughter Sandra and her son-in-law Chuck in Myrtle Beach. But Delores began showing signs of dementia. In 2019, she moved into a nursing home near Myrtle Beach.

Phillip and Delores

DELORES' TWO DAUGHTERS — AS CHILDREN AND ADULTS

Older daughter Sandra Lynn— Born 1954

Younger daughter Connie Bly — Born 1957

Mattie Lee

Mattie Lee Brittian was born in a log house in Harlan County, Kentucky in 1937. She was a pretty child and good natured, the youngest of the three Brittian sisters. Like her two older sisters, she was skinny, bordering on malnutrition. Her parents moved often from one small community to another, places with names like Gatliff, Nevisdale, Verne and Yaden. The coal mines where her father worked were in rural areas so the elementary schools she attended were usually small one-room school houses. She often had to walk from a half-mile to two miles to school. As an adolescent, she had two girl friends, Billie Rains and Opal Walters, who lived on the hill above her family. They were the only bright spot in an otherwise dull and unhappy life.

When Mattie was five years old, June left home while the World War II was going on. Her brothers had already left home to fight in the war: Jerry, Sam and "Did" had joined the Army; Jay had enlisted in the Marines. The boys received small paychecks and sent a little money to their parents every now and then. With June and her brothers away, her parents were able to manage a little better financially with only two children at home and there was less turmoil for Ruth and Mattie. But it was still a hard life for John and Rhoda financially.

When Mattie was about ten years old, her mother took a job with the railroad, cooking for the workmen who maintained the railroad's property in eastern Kentucky and Tennessee. When the workers had to be on the road for several days, Mattie was too young to be left by herself so Rhoda took her along when she left on Monday and returned on Friday. The problem was that Mattie missed a lot of school and didn't have anyone to play with.

After her older sister Ruth left home, Mattie was left alone with her parents. The three of them lived in grinding poverty on about $48.00/month. Mattie was a compliant child who managed to get along with her mother better than her two sisters but she was also unhappy. Her family was poor; the log house had no running water and she had few respectable clothes, only one decent dress to her name.

Her mother took her every Sunday to Siler's Chapel Church; one Sunday when she was about 10, she saw a man take hot coals out of the stove and handle them. She was terrified and miserable.

Like her sisters, Mattie was desperate to leave home. She was barely 13 when she met her second cousin, Aunt Mary's grandson, Gene Brown, at her Grandfather Smith's home in Verne. Mary had four children by her ex-husband Joe Brown. One of her daughters was Salatha Brown, Gene's mother. He was 26 years old with a checkered past. As a teenager, he had killed another teenager under suspicious circum-stances, leaving a stain on the family's name. To escape the turmoil, Mary brought Gene to live with her.

Gene and Mattie were both anxious to escape the critical eyes under which they lived so they decided to get married and leave home. Gene's grandmother Mary and his mother Salatha had always given in to his whims, so, when he told them that he and Mattie were going to get married, they eventually acquiesced. However, Mary neglected to tell her sister Rhoda, Mattie's mother, about the arrangement.

Aunt Mary and Gene took Mattie to Augusta, Georgia where they got married—she was barely 14. When Rhoda found out that Mary had helped Gene take Mattie to Georgia without her knowledge or consent, she almost collapsed in disbelief. Then she was furious. How could her daughter and sister do such a thing without consulting her?

It wasn't uncommon for girls in Eastern Kentucky to marry when they were 15 or 16. But 14! That was too young, even for a God-fearin' woman like Rhoda to abide. For one thing, she had never trusted her nephew and considered him a bad seed. Furthermore, she knew what he had done and she did not want her daughter's reputation, or her own, ruined by a bad marriage.

The Smith sisters were well-known for their strong wills and fierce tempers. When Mary and the newlyweds returned to Verne, Rhoda rushed to Mary's home to confront her sister and confirm what they had done behind her back. Rhoda suspected the Devil was working through Gene to corrupt her sister and daughter. She knew what to do. When they met on the front porch, Rhoda threatened to file white slavery charges against her sister for taking a minor across state lines.

For her part, Mary became so angry with her sister that she ran back inside the house and grabbed a pistol. She fired at her sister and barely missed her only because their brother Frazier knocked the gun aside just in time.

But Mattie's marriage soured quickly, lasting only about ten months. She soon realized she had only traded one miserable situation for another. As old timers used to say, they had neither a pot to piss in nor a window to throw it out of. So she and Gene were forced to stay with his mother Salatha who, besides being nosy, badgered Mattie constantly. Salatha was also controlling—she wouldn't even allow Mattie to mail a letter to her parents. Besides feeling like a prisoner, she and Gene quarreled and fought constantly.

Before long she made up her mind to leave Gene and seek a divorce. Her sister Delores and her husband Larry were living in Ypsilanti, Michigan. When they came back to Kentucky to visit their families, Mattie confided to her sister how unhappy and desperate she was to escape her dreadful life. Delores and Larry encouraged her to come to Michigan and stay with them while she pursued her divorce. They got Mattie's brother Jerry to take her to the Corbin bus station where she met Larry and Delores who took her to Ypsilanti.

At that time a young man named Preston Terry was living in Ypsilanti in low cost housing while working at General Motors. He had moved there from Lawrence County, Alabama. One weekend in June of 1954, he was killing time with some buddies on the lawn by Cunningham's Drug Store in a small strip mall in Ann Arbor. He saw a pretty young girl stroll by and enter the drug store.

It was love at first sight. Preston promptly turned to one of his buddies and announced, "I'm going to marry that girl!" He rushed into the drugstore, introduced himself and struck up a conversation.

In the drugstore there was a soda fountain where they served cokes and ice cream floats. She said she liked cherry cokes and that she had come there to get one. He bought one for her. He learned that she was Mattie Lee Brittian from Kentucky and that she had come to Ann Arbor with her sister Delores and her sister's husband Larry to escape an unpleasant situation at home. She was staying with Larry and Delores nearby in a little village made up of government houses.

They started dating when she was 17 and he was 20. They married in 1957. Throughout their marriage, Mattie and Preston were always devoted to each other, although sometimes, especially during the early years, their relationship was stormy with fierce fights. But they always made up and stuck together. It became their habit when they went to bed, even after a rancorous fuss during the day, to turn to the other and apologize for anything done or said that offended the other during the day and to say, "I love you" before they said "good night".

Throughout their lives, one constant all three sisters drew strength from was the loving relationship they shared with each other. Although the three sisters were married and often lived far apart, they remained close. They stayed in touch by phone, sharing their heartaches—and there were many—as well as their joys. Whenever they could manage it, all three of them and their spouses got together to talk, sing and cut up.

Their favorite song was "You Are My Sunshine", a popular song that was recorded in 1939 by Jimmy Davis and Charles Mitchell. The three of them especially loved the verse:

You are my sunshine, my only sunshine.

You make me happy when skies are gray.

You'll never know dear how much I love you.

Please don't take my sunshine away.

Preston

T he last third of the nineteenth century and the first half of the twentieth century were times of painful poverty for Southerners, but especially for black Americans. By the 1850s, most of the world's cotton was grown in the American south and spun and woven in the industrial cities of northern England. But the Civil War wrecked the South's economy by depriving it of the cheap, unskilled labor that supported its agrarian and colonial way of life. Plantation owners objected to ending slavery because they depended on slave labor to produce low-cost cotton. When President Lincoln issued the Emancipation Proclamation that freed black slaves in the southern states, it crippled the economies of states like Alabama. Higher prices for southern cotton destroyed the South's economy since European textile factories and merchants would turn to more affordable sources outside the South.

In the turbulent years of Reconstruction following the Civil War, the federal government tried to bring the vanquished southern states and their four million newly-freed slaves back into the United States. In 1878, however, federal troops withdrew from the South, returning it to local white rule, and the civil rights that blacks had been promised during Reconstruction were ignored under white rule in the south.

As support for reconstruction waned, white supremacy gradually regained its strangle hold on the South. The southern states managed to thwart the federal government's program of reconstruction by passing "Jim Crow" laws that enforced a legal system of racial segregation. The laws affected almost every aspect of daily Life, humiliated blacks and institutionalized an unfair legal system, inequality in education, and denial of suffrage.

Southern whites, hostile and bitter at losing the war, turned the freed black slaves into scapegoats by blaming them for the destruction of the south's economy. White southerners often reacted to the imposition of reconstruction by turning to violence. Many whites joined the Ku Klux Klan, an organization that terrorized black families, sometimes burning fiery crosses in front of their houses. Blacks were even beaten and murdered in lynchings that were widespread across the South.

Falling cotton prices on world markets, plus the negative effects of federal policies designed to rescue Southern planters at the expense of the workers, caused the decline of Southern cotton production and the massive collapse of Southern agricultural employment. In the 1920s cotton farming was further damaged by the infestation of boll weevils that had entered the U.S. from Mexico in the late 1800s. By the 1920s they had spread through all of the major cotton-producing areas in the country. The scale of their damage was breathtaking.

To make matters worse, the racial hatred of whites toward blacks was passed on from generation to generation. Besides rigid discrimination and segregation in the South, the brutal physical violence against blacks continued. The Jim Crow system endured for roughly 70 years until the civil rights movement in the 1960s supposidly ended it, but racism lingered on casting a dark pall of racism over America. Eventually, the plight of southern Blacks was largely forgotten in the north; blacks were segregated, discriminated against and condemned to live in poverty there as well.

As a result, job opportunities for Southerners continued to decline after the first World War as farmers—especially sharecroppers and tenant farmers—faced hard times. During those bleak years, black and white southerners were desperate to escape the grinding poverty that was rampant in the South. They moved in droves to industrial cities in the North where they could have better paying industrial jobs, home ownership, better educations, and the chance to influence public policy to their benefit through voting. Northern cities were also more racially tolerant and offered more personal freedom for black Americans than cities in the South.

This vast movement has been called the Great Migration because it was the largest internal migration in the history of the United States. More than 28 million southerners migrated to the North during the twentieth century; roughly 20 million whites and eight million southern blacks moved from the rural south to the urban North in a movement that gained momentum during World War I and lasted until 1970. This massive population shift profoundly transformed the twentieth-century United States politically, economically, socially, and culturally.

It was into these hard and tumultuous times that Preston Terry was born. Although he grew up steeped in the hateful racist culture of the South, it was not in his nature to be contemptuous or to feel superior to anyone, including black Americans. Some of the qualities that enabled him to rise above humble beginnings were a generous heart, an honest character, a positive attitude, a friendly disposition and the courage to speak up for what was right.

Raising cotton was a hard and unreliable way to make a living. In 1934, Lee Olean Terry, known as "L.O." to his friends, was a poor, white tenant farmer in northeastern Alabama. "L.O." was a hard worker and a strict father who expected his wife and children to help out on the farm. His wife Florence, a big-boned woman with long, black hair, whose family moved from Oklahoma to Lawrence County, Alabama when she was a child, came from sturdy Cherokee Indian stock. She helped the men pick cotton after she cooked breakfast and only quit to fix lunch or dinner. Even so, she could pick more than most men: 300 pounds of cotton in a day.

That same year Florence delivered the seventh of their twelve children into the world. The baby boy's name was Preston. As a teenager, he was a curious lad, always eager to figure out how things worked, and a hard worker too. He was sensible and responsible but not in a serious way because he had an engaging sense of humor. Nor was he bashful. His Pap claimed he would talk to a fence post.

When he was eight years old, his father sent Preston into the fields to pick cotton with his older brothers. That didn't sit too well with the youngster and he decided after three or four years of picking cotton that there had to be a better kind of work to do. Picking cotton was a hard way to make a living—the taller you were, the more you had to stoop over making your back hurt—and it didn't pay well. The brutal working conditions drained the life out of you: clothes became soaked in sweat in summer, prickly cotton bolls bloodied fingers, and the work was exhausting.

Every summer, well into his teenage years and decked out in an old straw hat, Preston dragged a six foot long heavy burlap sack behind him down the long rows of cotton. The more cotton he picked, the heavier the sack became.

After a few seasons he was able to pick 150 pounds in a day—a seasoned picker could fill maybe two bags with 150 pounds of cotton each. Cotton pickers were paid by the pound and he usually received $1.50 to $2.00 for a hundred pounds picked. His fingers bled and stayed sore from being pricked by the sharp tips of the cotton bolls.

Lunch usually consisted of canned kraut, fried potatoes, corn bread and maybe some weak tea to drink. After supper, the picked cotton had to be taken to the gin in a wagon pulled by a team of horses.

For two years, Preston pondered his future. He listened to his father, his mother, and his older brothers and lived the same hard lives they endured. He studied his older sisters Inez and Othella, married and no longer living with their parents, but still struggling to make ends meet. He was disturbed when he realized most of the older farmers living in Lawrence County would have to work until they died.

By the time he was sixteen, he had become keenly aware of his likely prospects for the same hard life as an adult. He was also frustrated because his obligations on the farm interfered with getting an education. It was obvious to him that, without a good education, his vocational potential was limited. He hated the uncertainty of farming and the ongoing lack of financial security it entailed. It would soon be planting time and he was dreading it. *I can't go on like this*, he thought. He decided he would leave home after the next crop was in and look for a job in Michigan like many other black and white Southerners.

By the 1950s, the southern economy was taking a turn for the worse. The South was no longer the dominant source of cotton, even within the United States. The southeastern cotton states became minor producers as the cotton belt shifted west. It was the last straw. Although many poor whites experienced some discrimination, they were compelled to migrate not so much to escape persecution as to seek economic opportunity.

For each of us, there comes a pivotal moment in our life when we must make a critical decision about the direction our life will take; for some of us, it happens several times. That moment can seem insignificant or even go unnoticed at the time, but it is the point when our life takes on a new direction. It can be the result of a hasty decision or one that comes only after prolonged and careful deliberation.

In 1950, when Preston Terry was 16, he made the pivotal decision that changed the course of his life. One damp evening that spring, the Terry family was gathered around the kitchen table after dinner. Pap Terry was discussing the preparations they would soon need to make to plant the next crop of cotton. Preston's older sisters Inez and Othella and his brother Wallace had all married and moved to Ypsilanti, Michigan to find jobs in the automobile industry. Only his brothers Leldon and Hollis were still living at home.

Preston had dreaded bringing up to his parents and his brothers his decision to leave. He felt guilty because he knew his leaving would make it harder on the rest of his family.

Finally he got his nerve up. "Hey, y'all, listen up. I've got something to tell you."

Slightly irritated but somewhat curious, his father put his pencil down. He was trying to decide what he needed to buy in town the next day and he didn't like being interrupted when he was trying to work something out. "Okay, quiet everybody. Preston's got something to tell us," he said, rolling his eyes.

"I just wanted to tell you all that I'm plannin' on leavin' Alabama and goin' up north. Othella says there's jobs up there that pay a lot better than pickin' cotton and are easier on your back." He paused to gauge their reaction.

His brothers Leldon and Hollis stared at him and then at their father with their mouths open. "You're not serious, are you, Preston?" Hollis asked. You're just pullin' our leg, ain't you?"

"No, I ain't, Hollis. I'm really goin'."

"Are you gonna' go to Michigan and stay with Othella?" Leland asked.

His father studied Preston without saying a word. Usually his father would not say much at first when he was chewing over something, but when he did speak it was like a dam breaking. This time was different. Another one of his family was leaving and he didn't know what to do about it.

Preston looked at his brother and then his father. "I wrote Othella and she said I could stay with her and Arthur until I find a job."

He noticed his mother was on the verge of crying. Her family was coming apart. "I don't want you to go, Preston. You're too young to be goin' out on your own. Do you want to worry me to death?"

"No, Momma, I don't, but I have to go. You know I'll miss you. And Pap too." He looked from one to the other of them and wiped the wetness from his eyes. He was feeling guilty and missing his family already. "All of you, I'll miss you all." There, he'd said it and now he had to go.

Like many other Southerners, for Preston Terry, it was time to go. He joined that great migration to the North to find a job and a better life. He left home after the crops were in and went to join his brothers and sisters and many other Southerners who had already left the south behind. When he boarded a Greyhound bus for the long and tiring trip to small town Ypsilanti, Michigan, he became part of that great migration to the North.

Othella and Authur lived in low cost housing. Their house was small. As soon as Preston arrived, he realized that he had to get his own place. When he was settled in, he went looking for a job. In a few days, he found one driving a taxi cab.

With the steady money from that job, he was eventually able to rent a small place of his own while he kept looking for a job that would offer better pay and benefits. A few months later, he landed a job at General Motors and joined the United Auto Workers Union.

He was making more money and things were looking up when he experienced another stroke of good luck. He met the love of his life in Mattie Lee Brittian, an attractive young lady from Kentucky. Before long he convinced her to move in with him and together they enjoyed the happiest time of their lives. Mattie found a job working at first for a plastics company and eventually at the Chrysler plant in Ypsilanti making $4.00 per hour. With two incomes, they were able to save some money.

In 1957, while working for GM, Preston was drafted into the Army and stationed at Ft. Louis in Olympia, Washington for two years. In June of 1959, as soon as he was discharged from the Army, they took a bus to see his parents in Somerville, Alabama. After they recovered from the trip, Preston's sister Evelyn took them to pick up his car and they drove just across the state line to Iuka, Mississippi and got married on June 14, with only $14 to their name.

After driving back to Ypsilanti, Preston had just one dollar in his wallet. He went back to work at GM but still didn't make much money. After he married Mattie, he continued to drive a taxi part time for the next 20 years. For the first few years of their marriage, it was hard to make ends meet. But they worked hard and eventually bought a small house in Ypsilanti.

The winters were harsh in southern Michigan and, as the years passed, Preston felt the red clay fields of Alabama pulling at him, drawing him back to his roots. It's human nature—and a blessed thing it is—that we tend to forget the harsh experiences of our younger years while clinging to an oft' embellished memory of a kinder and simpler time. Maybe it was that memory that beckoned to him so strongly.

In 1973, Preston and Mattie bought some land for the house they planned to build. In 1982, they had a stroke of incredibly good luck when Chrysler moved their plant to Huntsville, Alabama allowing Mattie to work in that plant which was close to the house they were having built. Preston had to continue working at the GM plant in Ypsilanti for a year and a half until he could retire.

After he retired from GM on January 1, 1984, he and Mattie lived in a small house in Huntsville. Later in the year they moved into their new home, an attractive rancher on a wooded lot in rural Somerville, near Huntsville in northern Alabama, not far from where he had grown up.

In 1984, life in Alabama was far better than it was in the 50s. The standard of living was higher. The Civil Rights Act of 1964 made life much more tolerable for black Americans although latent discrimination continued to smolder in less obvious ways. Farming was still important but factories were moving from the north to the south offering better paying jobs.

Gradually through hard work and frugality, Preston and Mattie Lee realized the love and security they both longed for. By the time they were both retired, they had achieved the American dream. Throughout their married life, they remained faithful to each other while enjoying a comfortable retirement. Now in their 80s, they remain happily together in Somerville, still devoted to each other, while confronting the health challenges of their senior years with an enduring sense of humor and peace of mind.

Cunningham's Drugstore in Ann Arbor, Michigan 1953

Saying Goodbye

His father was an alcoholic, abusive and unaffectionate toward his wife at times, and harsh toward his two sons. In spite of his father's example, Raymond never took to alcohol and did not smoke. For whatever reason, he never embraced religion, except for a short period during his later years.

Like all of us, Raymond was far from perfect but he loved his three children and was always there when they needed help. The hard part of being a father is loving your wife and children and being there for them day in and day out, even during the hard times when you don't know how you're going to support them. In that Raymond was faithful. He and June had terrible fights from time to time but they always got back together.

Raymond was not Sammy's biological father, but he was truly Sammy's father in every way that counted. His and Sammy's natures were different in many ways, but Sammy loved and respected his stepfather. Raymond was the only father Sammy knew and before long Ramond adopted him.

In his mid eighties, Raymond began to show signs of dementia and panic attacks that broke his children's hearts. In early 2014, he became seriously ill unexpectedly. In spite of a strong constitution and his doctor's efforts, his condition worsened until he was near death.

His children lost their father on October 18, 2014 when he was 87. Thankfully, he died at home. Traditionally, Raymond and his family had always come together to celebrate Christmas. But the Christmas of 2014 was not joyful. It was the first one without Raymond. His wife and children sorely missed him and his children remembered him by reading the following letter after their meal:

Dec. 25, 2014

Dear Dad,
This will be our first Christmas without you. You loved Christmas, good food and being with your family. It was always a fun time and full of love. Because of that, Christmas was always special to us. We still remember the magic of Christmas and the gifts you and Mom got for us.

You were a young man when you took on the responsibilities of a family; it wasn't easy but you built a home for us with your own hands, supported us through recessions and showed us lots of unconditional love. You taught us to work hard, to be honest and respectful and that there was more to life than having money.

We remember fondly all the years our family met around the kitchen table as children and adults to share a meal at Christmas. We remember all the times you helped us out when we were going through rough times. You loved having a garden and, as a farmer, you were among the best. You always had a big garden so you could share with all of us and our families. And you never threw anything away. These are some of the things we will never forget.

So here we are again on Christmas day, still missing you. We celebrate your time with us here on Earth and we rejoice in your spirit and your kindness. You had a pretty long life of 87 years, but we would have loved to have had you around longer. It's not the same without you, but we'll always remember all the things you taught us.

We suspect you are up in heaven looking down on us. You were a dear friend, a loving husband, and a great father. Thank you for being there for us.

We've never begged for miracles,
But today just one would do:
To hear the front door open
And to see our Dad walk through.

We miss you, Dad.

Merry Christmas!
Sam, Smiley, Pam

Raymond passed away just 18 months before June. She had been married to him for 69 years, ever since she was 20 years old. They had worked hard all of their lives to pay for a nicely furnished home that would be a good place for the family to live. Since she had grown up in a small log home, it meant a lot for her to have a brick home with a nice kitchen and modern conveniences.

He was a good man who in some ways was dealt a bad hand in life. His three adult children missed him terribly. He was always there to help them when they needed him. More than two years after his death, it was still difficult for them to accept that he was gone. Losing both their parents so close together left them reeling from the loss and struggling with depression because they were a close family.

Her children lost their mother bit by bit. Symptoms of dementia began to appear by June's 85th birthday in 2010. It was obvious her memory was slipping. She sometimes asked the same question several times.

The next four years were increasingly difficult as her health issues worsened. She had suffered from macular degeneration for several years and her eyesight was failing. She could still walk unsteadily, but not far. She could not distinguish night from day. In 2014, her husband Raymond died. By that time she was no longer able to live alone.

June's daughter Pam brought their mother to live with her and tried to take care of her but it was too much for her. June required constant attention: since she had trouble sleeping, she tended to continue talking after she went to bed. Sometimes she would wander through the house at night, calling out, "Mommy, where are you?" She went through a suspicious phase when she thought people, even Pam, were stealing her clothes. After two or three days Pam would be exhausted.

June was 89 when she had to go into a nursing home. Her dementia had worsened and her overall health was declining. The first nursing home she went into was a disappointing experience. The staff left her sitting alone for hours and only seemed to care about finding some excuse to charge more for her residency.

What a terrible adjustment going into a nursing home like that must have been for her! It's hard to imagine how alone she must have felt, spending most of every day cooped up in a small room and sleeping by herself at night in a strange place. Her children often found her curled up on her small bed holding the stuffed teddy bear they had brought her from home.

During her first few months in the nursing home, she was quite lucid and capable of robust conversations and displays of affection. Many times she told her children she would gladly lay down her life for them. It was obvious she meant it and that her children were the most important part of her life.

Sometimes she would plead with her children to take her home with them. She would ask pointedly in a softly pleading voice, "Why can't I stay with you?" That would break their hearts.

Her children would try to explain that she needed medical care and someone to be with her 24/7, but they could tell she didn't understand. She couldn't understand where she was. She felt abandoned. She was miserable; her whole life had been turned upside down.

While she was in that nursing home, her mental and physical conditions declined at a quickening pace. Her dementia progressed into Alzheimer's. She struggled to remember her children's names and stopped pleading to go home with them. Yet, she still felt a strong connection to them and always beamed whenever they came to see her. She remained affectionate and loving until the end.

Within six months she was unable to walk using a walker. In less than a year, she became confined to a wheelchair as her balance and coordination worsened until she was no longer able to walk safely. She did fall several times, hurting herself badly. Besides that, she became incontinent, sometimes unable to reach the toilet and use it without help.

After almost a year in the first nursing home, things were not going well. Although her care was rather expensive, the staff was not particularly attentive. Sometimes June was not given her medications or was left sitting by herself for long periods of time.

No matter how badly she felt, she rarely complained. But sometimes she would declare, "Life's the shits and then you die!" and laugh heartily. That was her opinion of life. Nobody knew where she came up with it, but for the last few years of her life that was her mantra. Perhaps it was an expression of the cold cynicism she had embraced about life early on because of the hardships and disappointments she had experienced.

Frustrated, her children found another nursing home where the staff was friendlier and more attentive. It was less expensive, although not quite as nice as the first one. But June was happier there.

In spite of all the change she had to endure, she kept her sense of humor and loved to cut up with the new nursing home staff. She loved them and they treated her with kindness. Her children never forgot how her eyes lit up when they came to visit her.

During her last few months, June was unable to feed herself. She lost her appetite. Eventually, her memory failed her and she forgot about her home. She forgot about her husband and never mentioned him. She was unable to remember anyone except her children and eventually not even them. She was totally alone, surrounded by strangers. She had lost control over every part of her life.

June's steady decline laid over her children a deep and abiding cover of sadness. Clearly she had suffered enough. Yet how could they give her up? She was tired and nearly blind. The extent of her life was no more than a small room with a single bed, a bathroom and a closet. There would be no more walks outside, no more Sunday meals with her family, no more trips to the grocery store, no more visits with friends. Only a small dim room and a monotonous, dull existence remained.

The realization that her life had come full circle had a sad and painful impact on her children. She began her adult life with practically nothing and she ended it the same way, with little more than the love of her small family. In her room, besides her bed, her only personal belongings were a chifforobe, a night stand, a rocking chair, a side chair and a teddy bear—not even a phone or TV. That didn't seem fair.

For the children, selling their parents' home and personal belongings was a long and painful process. It included their father's tools, their mother's kitchen items, their knickknacks and mem-orabilia—all the small, personal things that gave their home its special character. Some of the hardest things to give up were their parents' bedroom furniture: their bed, dresser, chest of drawers, side tables and rocker. These were things that would be sold for only a fraction of their worth while priceless to the children.

It is said that life isn't fair. Her oldest son believed that and said it himself many times. Every time he came to see her, he thought it when he spotted her—small, frail and utterly alone—sitting in her wheelchair or lying on her small bed. Seeing her like that hurt him and made him angry. He found no comfort in religion. *What was the point of it all?* he wondered.

Wednesday March 23, 2016. Victorian Square Nursing Home. Rockwood, Tennessee. At 9:00 a.m. her older son Sam sat in her room, feeling unmoored and hollowed out inside as he witnessed her struggle to breathe. She couldn't talk. She lay on her side in a fetal position— unaware of him—her breaths coming quick and shallow. A feeling of panic settled over him; he was desperate to do something to comfort her, to ease her pain. But what?

He closed his eyes and thought, *My oh my, how fast the years have gone by! Now our roles are reversed. Once I was the helpless one, now she is. I owe my life to this brave and wonderful woman but I can do nothing to save her. She could have easily given me up in her time of need and eased her burden when she was young and vulnerable. But she refused to do that, no matter what. Now there is absolutely nothing I can do; I am powerless to rescue her and ease her pain.*

The fact that he couldn't talk to her made him want to scream in desperate protest but at whom? Or what? He couldn't tell her how much he loved her or thank her for what she had done for her children. He felt such pain and anger that it seemed his heart was being ripped out of his body. He felt utterly helpless and confused: *this isn't the way her life should end—she deserves better than this.*

For most of her life, she had been strong and independent. Now she was small and helpless. He lovingly stroked her hair as his eyes filled with tears. Her birthday was the month before; she had turned 91. But there was nothing left to celebrate.

June had been under the care of hospice for almost six weeks. One day the hospice nurse warned her children before they entered her room that she would pass within a few hours. They were crushed. They couldn't bear to give her up in spite of the fact that she had said many times she wanted to *"go on"*. It was her way of saying she didn't want to live any longer—she was ready to meet death.

They had known for many months that this dreaded day was drawing near. Still they were unprepared, fully unable to deal with the loss of their mother. Each of them had to get away to collect their thoughts about how their lives would change without her. When they returned a few hours later, two nurses and a staffer were gathered in her room.

June was gone. She had passed just minutes before. Her children felt ashamed and bitter—and more helpless than ever. In the end, she had died alone with no one able to comfort her. Her three children, whom she loved more than anything else in the world and who loved her more than anyone else in the world, were not there with her in her final moments.

Losing their mother bit by bit over a period of years was hard. *It would have been a kinder death*, they agreed, *if she had died like Walter, quickly and unexpectedly, so that her suffering would be over quickly.* For her children the pain of losing their mother would never be over.

How do you say goodbye to the woman who gave you life, nurtured you and loved you unconditionally? The next few months were painful as the three children grieved over their loss and tried to come to terms with how their lives had been transformed by the loss of both parents. *What an incredible woman she was. What a loving spirit she had. In spite of a difficult childhood of neglect and faltering love from her own mother, she was always patient, kind and attentive to her own children in every way.*

There is a bond between mother and child that often transcends all other relationships. In the months after her passing, the more they thought about her, the more they regretted how little they actually knew about the personal and intimate details of her life, especially the sacrifices she had made for them.

They thought about their mother's generation—four older brothers and two younger sisters. All of her brothers and both parents were dead. Only her two younger sisters, Delores and Mattie, and Mattie's husband Preston were still alive. It came as a revelation that they were stunningly ignorant about near relatives on both sides of the family.

Somehow over the years they had failed to coax her into revealing all the memories that would have helped them appreciate what a remarkable woman their mother was. In truth, they had heard only bits and pieces about her life because there was so much she had "packed away" in the attic of her mind and didn't want to bring out for all to see.

Sadly, it was much the same on their father's side of the family. There was precious little talk about Raymond's kin. His father Walter's background was a mystery. Few words were ever spoken about his mother Mary and her siblings. His older brother Kenneth was killed in 1944 at the Battle of Normandy when he was barely 20 years old. No one ever talked about him. Perhaps the falling-out between father and son was too painful—or shameful. There probably were things that would have been confusing for children to hear.

How many women are like June, Delores and Mattie who traveled a rough and winding path from the day they were born? Yet, somehow they made the most of the life they had and still turned it to the good.

When June and Delores' children were grown, they came to realize how fortunate they were to have had the parents they did. Their parents were flawed, far from perfect as all of us are, and ill-prepared for the responsibilities of parenting, but they did the best they could with what they had. They were always loving and helpful, never abusive or harsh.

Perhaps the success of a parent's life is reflected best in the lives of their children who mourn their passing, remember them fondly and honor them by never straying from the straight path they were set upon. It is fitting to celebrate our parents' lives and honor them for nurturing and mentoring us. June and Delores' children will always remember their parent's example because they brought love, joy and meaning to their lives. Their parents taught them that what matters is not how much you take but how much you give.

Final Thoughts by the Author

Perhaps the success of a parent's life is reflected best in the lives of their children who mourn their passing, remember them fondly and honor them by never straying from the straight path they were set upon. It is fitting to celebrate our parents' lives and honor them for nurturing and mentoring us.

As June and Raymond's children, the three of us will always remember our parents' example because they brought love, joy and meaning to our lives. They taught us that what matters is not how much you have or take but how much you give.

After losing our parents, Ken, Pam and I have been forced to question more profoundly what life is about, who we are and what we must do with the remainder of our lives. We have learned by observing our parents' example that time is the measure of life. Because time is fleeting, life is precious. We must use the time allotted to us wisely so we do not squander our life.

In one sense, the loss of our mother and father was a wake-up call for us. We can no longer ignore the fact that we ourselves are older now and that we too will someday, in the not so distant future, face our own mortality. Our parents have given us a preview of what awaits us; in time we too will lose our independence, become inactive and with each passing year become less relevant to a changing world.

The three of us have remained close over the years as we have to our mother's sisters Delores and Mattie who are well into their 80s. We dread the time when we will lose one another and our aunts.

Although our parents were woefully unschooled in the ways of a modern, fast-changing world, they were incredibly understanding and loving human beings. We were also blessed to have had Aunt Mattie and Uncle Preston who, although having no children themselves, loved us and treated us like their own. Their love and encouragement sustain us as we grow older.

Now the story of the three Brittian sisters from Harlan County in Kentucky has been told, but it is wildly incomplete. With so many intimate details lost to time, what is written here reveals only a fleeting glimpse of the full measure of their lives. It is like trying to know a man by studying his shadow. Their lives were so much more than what is described in this small book.

Nevertheless, let us celebrate all the brave and free-spirited women everywhere who are able to survive and even flourish under the most trying conditions and in the most difficult of times. Each one is like a wildflower, beautiful and exotic in her own way.

If you're a woman reading this book, perhaps you're one of them.

June with Granddaughter Michelle   Delores Ruth

How seldom the world is blessed with women so beautiful who love as much as these.

– Sobra Konin

Mattie Lee